THE
HEALING POWER
of *Faery*

THE
HEALING POWER
of *Faery*

Working with Elementals and Nature Spirits to
Soothe the Body and Soul

EDAIN McCOY

PROVENANCE
P R E S S

Avon, Massachusetts

Published by
Provenance Press, an imprint of Adams Media,
an F+W Publications Company
57 Littlefield Street, Avon, MA 02322. U.S.A.
www.adamsmedia.com

ISBN 13: 978-1-59869-809-1
ISBN 10: 1-59869-809-5

Printed in Canada.

J I H G F E D C B A

Library of Congress Cataloging-in-Publication Data
available from publisher.

This publication is designed to provide accurate and authoritative information with
regard to the subject matter covered. It is sold with the understanding that the publisher
is not engaged in rendering legal, accounting, or other professional advice. If legal advice
or other expert assistance is required, the services of a competent professional person
should be sought.
—From a *Declaration of Principles* jointly adopted by a Committee of the
American Bar Association and a Committee of Publishers and Associations

Many of the designations used by manufacturers and sellers to distinguish their products are claimed as trademarks. Where those designations appear in this book and
Adams Media was aware of a trademark claim, the designations have been printed with
initial capital letters.

The Healing Power of Faery is intended as a reference volume only, not as a medical
manual. In light of the complex, individual, and specific nature of health problems, this
book is not intended to replace professional medical advice. The ideas, procedures, and
suggestions in this book are intended to supplement, not replace, the advice of a trained
medical professional. Consult your physician before adopting the suggestions in this
book, as well as about any condition that may require diagnosis or medical attention.
The author and publisher disclaim any liability arising directly or indirectly from the
use of this book.

This book is available at quantity discounts for bulk purchases.
For information, please call 1-800-289-0963.

ALSO BY EDAIN MCCOY

Advanced Witchcraft

Astral Projection for Beginners

Bewitchments

Celtic Myth and Magick

Celtic Women's Spirituality

Enchantments

Entering the Summerland

How to Do Automatic Writing

If You Want to Be a Witch

Karmic & Past Life Tarot

Magick and Rituals of the Moon

Making Magick

Mountain Magick

The Ninth Hallows

Ostara

A Witch's Guide to Faery Folk

The Sabbats

Spellworking for Covens

Three Witches Dead & the Last One Said . . .

The Witches' Coven

Witta

content

with grateful thanks . . .

To all friends and partners of faery, and to those who took time to share with me their stories of faery, helping to make this book possible; including: Ron Cordes, Mystral of FPG, Mike, Christopher Penczak, Margie McArthur, Rhiannon Skye, Morganna Feyraven, Breanna WinDancer, Ann Marie of FPG, Beth, Chris, and Jackie in Alabama; Erik McBride, D.D.; and my amazing agent, Denise Dumars.

A unique nod of thanks goes to one special fey friend—Thomas O'Shaughnessy—a man who now "knows better."

introduction
Tearing Through the Rip in Manannan MacLir's Cloak

I first saw faeries when I was six years old. At the time my family lived in a parsonage in an older neighborhood in South Bend, Indiana. We lived next door to a genteel old English lady who maintained a spectacular English garden beside her large house. One beautiful spring night, I was leaning on my bedroom windowsill looking out over the expanse of garden between our parsonage and the neighbor's house when I noticed movement around a circular bed of flowers.

The beings I saw there were translucent. I thought I was seeing ghosts, but then realized the creatures I was watching were not human enough to be ghosts. There were five or six of them and all appeared to be female. Their long gowns seemed to be part of their bodies from the waist up, but trailed like a hazy mist as they fell toward the grass. I noticed a hint of gossamer wings—a cliché, I know, but that's what they looked like to me—with no clear demarcation between their bodies and the air around them.

Although their bodies were those of well-formed adults, I estimated them to be no more than three feet tall. Their eyes were large and entrancing, and their ears seemed overlarge beneath thick long hair that swayed as they danced clockwise around the flower bed.

Two weeks after I witnessed what I know now to be faeries playing in my next-door neighbor's English garden, my grandmother came to visit. She gave me a book called *The Happy Easter Storybook* in which I saw a drawing of the same beings I'd spotted in the garden only weeks before. After all these years and twenty-five moves to different homes, I still have that tattered book, and I pull it out occasionally to remind myself why I believe in faeries.

This book is not your standard how-to text. Faery is a subject that cannot be contained in a how-to, step-by-step format. Because I want this book to reach as wide an audience as possible, some of you who already have a working relationship with faery and are seeking only to deepen it, may find your eyes crossing at the beginning chapters of this book. You know how faeries appear, you understand their diversity, and you accept them as they present themselves to you.

The Legend of Manannan MacLir's Cloak

One of the most famous tales in Celtic mythology is that of Manannan MacLir's Cloak. In it, a faery beauty known as Fand, who lives beneath a bejeweled Irish lake, falls deeply in love with a human man, the Red Branch warrior hero, Cuchulain. The sea God, King Manannan MacLir, watched the couple try to mesh their two worlds into one in which they could flourish both as individuals and as a couple. But he saw only disaster as both human and faery continued to war. The values of each race were different, and each saw the other as an enemy who threatened his or her very existence.

Saddened by what he witnessed, but believing he was acting in the best interest of all, the King allowed Fand and Cuchulain to say their farewells at the edge of Fand's lake, on a place that could not be said to be either earth or water. Manannan raised his magickal cloak between the couple. Fand returned to her lake and Cuchulain to his warriors. The memory of one another and one another's worlds were erased from their minds.

Why Should Humans Reunite with Faery?

Why does such a wide chasm still exist between the human world and the world of faery? Why are we separate from faery, unable to reach physically into the overlap of our worlds without exerting tremendous effort? Why is it even difficult to meet on "neutral ground" in the astral plane that lies between our two distinct worlds? Why were faery lost to us and we lost to them for so many centuries? Why have we stopped believing? And why should humans and faeries now seek to interact with one another again?

We need only look at the present state of the world to see that two different human cultures are not always able to live in harmony with one another. It's no surprise, then, that beings from two different realms might find peaceful interaction difficult. Although many New Agers, nature lovers, children, and Pagans today are seeking to reconnect with the multifaceted realm of faery, it would be wrong to suggest that we and the fey are trusted pals. There will always be people who don't believe in faery, just as there will always be faeries who do not like or wish to interact with humans. Fortunately, history shows us that sometimes old foes can become new allies. We know from experience that two groups united in one cause are much stronger than two separate groups trying to achieve the same ends on their own.

Our races exist in close proximity. Humans live on the earth plane; faeries live between earth and the astral plane, which overlaps our world even though it is not usually visible to us. Learning to live in peace with our neighbors is an important goal, and one this book encourages.

Through *The Healing Power of Faery,* you will learn to travel between our world and the world of faery, which is not often seen during our normal waking consciousness. You will learn to respect otherworlds and their inhabitants, and you will share information beneficial to all. The process of healing the self, others, the faery, and Mother Earth will be the primary focus of your beginner's quest. Faery is more than a cute story in a children's book and more than a cauldron of gold at the end of a rainbow. It is unselfish spiritual power, an energy that never dies, but merely changes form in accordance with our healing needs.

Faeries and Healing

It is common knowledge that many modern medicines were derived from plant parts. Shamans have always relied on a healing plant to tell them of its healing aspects. For tens of thousands of years, this provided humankind's only medical care.

The class of faeries known as nature spirits are the sentient power or soul of a plant, flower, herb, or tree. Early tribal shamans discovered they could use their skills in moving between worlds to contact these spirits of nature and ask for guidance in the healing arts. Sometimes the treatment would be astral, or the essence of the plant being mentally transferred to the patient. Other times the faery spirit would tell the shaman to make a sachet of various plant parts and keep it on or near the body of the person in need of healing. Still others would give prescriptions for live dosing for those who were sick.

The shaman also watched animals to see what they ate or rejected when ill. These examples provided further clues to healing. Even today, a shaman who notes an animal's attraction to a specific set of plants when ill will later go to the nature spirit to discover if the plant's power would also work on humans, and, if so, how it should be given.

This is no different than a medium calling up the spirit of a deceased relative to ask questions. It is always possible the spirit will be able to shed new light on a dark situation. Other times the inquest fails because being dead does not make anyone smart or skillful in the healing arts.

The key to healing using the art of faery shamanism is to go to the spirit of the plant itself, or to go into the wild reaches of a physical or astral woodland, and ask for guidance. More often than not, the shaman is called to a particular plant. When a sample of the plant is taken to a botanist or other plant expert, it contains healing properties in some part of itself.

Be aware that nontoxic plants can have poisonous roots, petals, or seeds. Much study on your part, and much guidance from the faery, will be needed to master this craft.

Keep in mind that the extinction of plant species is a serious concern to faery and humanity alike. As we continue to destroy the natural world in favor of pastureland or development, we are killing off various plants, trees, and wildflowers, at the rate of hundreds per day. There should be no one living today who is not aware that our life support is coming from a delicate ecosystem. Oftentimes we have no idea what we've made extinct or what healing powers those now extinct plants could have offered to us. The only way to gain a little of this power back is to take a shamanic journey into the faery realm, as will be taught in another chapter, and make requests. Nature spirits who have nowhere to live on our planet will transition to another world, just as human spirits do. Contacting the "dead" nature spirit or faery in its own otherworld is the best hope we have to reconnect with long forgotten healing energies, perhaps even being told of a location where the shaman can find a few remaining plants and rescue them from extinction.

The most important point to remember is that we and faery can assist one another in our mutual quest to heal the earth and each other. Each race of beings can help the other do what it cannot do by itself. By merging our individual healing energies into a dynamic force, we can aid all who depend on Mother Earth for their existence. When a living person travels to and from the faery realm—or any of the many other-world realms—to bring back answers to problems or medical advice for the sick, this person is walking the traditional path of the community shaman, one of the oldest spiritual practices on Earth.

Becoming a Faery Shaman

In this book we will explore the safest ways for someone who is neither a botanist, skilled healer, experienced faery shaman, nor a licensed medical doctor to begin working with plant spirits, as an initiated, yet still a beginning student of faery shamanism. You will start to become familiar with many types of nature spirits and the help they can provide to you. You will learn to concoct magic spells to heal problems in your life. You will discover how to work with the awesome powers of nature, and understand how nature's powers are working through you, with the common goal of healing those things most dear to us: our bodies, spirits, emotions, and our Earth. You'll begin walking between the worlds of faery and human at this critical juncture in time.

Since the time known in English language literature as the Celtic Renaissance (late nineteenth century), faeries and curious humans have been ripping holes in that old cloak of Manannan MacLir's, sometimes even stepping through the hole to frolic for a while in the other's home-land. To everyone's surprise, they return with knowledge of another world they can use in their own for the benefit of all. This book urges you to willfully rip through Manannan MacLir's threadbare cloak to reclaim a partnership that never should have been broken, and to renew an old friendship in service to a higher purpose.

The average student of faery shamanism should have no trouble fol-lowing these basic guidelines, and will begin to build new ones of their own. Those who wish to use linear thinking, have all details spelled out for them, expect wisdom on a silver platter, or who think they need a technical manual to work and play in the world of faery will find those doors forever closed. There is no "one right way," nor is there adequate language to describe many rituals and experiences. They have to be undertaken by the seeker who refuses to look at the world in black and white, or even in the spectral colors. Faery shamanism, like all occult arts that take us to otherworlds and back, is an intuitive path. What works for one shaman may not work for another. We share our knowledge with one another in hopes that others will experience the wonderful worlds of magick we have experienced, and through that personal experience we move from knowledge (an idea or commonly accepted standard) to wisdom (accepting and living in harmony with our learning).

Healing is as much an intuitive art as it is a chemical change, such as we expect in taking modern medicines. Think back on all your past visits to your doctor. How many times was he or she baffled by some physical problem you presented? How many times did he or she try a variety of techniques to make you well? How often were you referred on to a so-called specialist?

If you approach this book as you would a computer manual or a doctor's diagnostic computer program, you are destined to fail in your quest to be a faery shaman. There simply are few carved-in-stone pro-cedures or rules outside of the accepted etiquette faery asks of us. If you wish to walk the path of the faery shaman, be ready to see without your eyes, feel without your hands, smell without your nose, talk with-out your mouth, and decide your next stop without your analytical left brain chattering distractions.

1

Who Are the Faeries?

Semantics! The great stumbling stone of every spiritual adventurer. If we could just find a way to express our experiences and otherworld encounters without words, our quest for enlightenment would proceed with greater ease. The truth is that the vocabulary we have in our human language to express our interactions with the otherworldly beings falls far short in its capability to convey those interactions with any accuracy to those who have not shared similar otherworld experiences.

It would seem reasonable that discussing the faeries, or "the fey" as we often call them, would be one of our easiest world-to-world translations because we live on planes overlapping one another. Yet it is this very closeness that produced the grudges and outright hatred between our peoples, and that still strains our attempts at reconnecting.

Opinions differ about who or what faeries are. Some students of metaphysics believe faeries are angels who appear in a guise we don't recognize as angelic. Some think faeries are manifestations of the nine muses of Greco-Roman mythology. Others consider faeries dangerous creatures, linked to a class of underworld demons.

Faery Tales

"By some accounts, faeries evolved from the Picts, the indigenous people who lived in Ireland and parts of Britain before the Saxons invaded the Isles. Morgan Le Fay, King Arthur's sister, may have

been a beansidhe [pronounced ban-shee] or faery woman. Another theory suggests that faeries are the energetic prototypes from which humans developed. These beings look like beautiful people whose forms are virtually perfect." —Skye Alexander, *The Everything®
Wicca and Witchcraft Book, 2nd Edition*

The species of faery are many. Some are small, some are giants. Some are deities, some are the souls of nature. Some are the spirits of a specific place. Some are no doubt ethnic, others are mere shadows of the memory of magickal races of people who came before us on the earth plane. The nature spirits, and their rulers, are the faery we seek for healing partnerships. Even though they still enjoy a good game and harmless fun with us, these are among the most reliable, approachable, and like-minded of faery.

Identifying Faeries

The phenomenon of faery spans the entire globe, and faeries are a part of the folklore of every civilization—even in cultures that have been isolated from outside contact for hundreds of years. Such widespread acceptance of faeries from thousands of cultures would lead us to expect broad differences in the powers and appearances of faeries and nature spirits. To the contrary, the folk beliefs and practices surrounding faery temperament and faery behavior contain startling similarities.

Any plant spirit you encounter is likely to be a faery who contains within itself the magical and medicinal powers of that plant. They are less playful than other nature spirits, are not able to move too far away from their host plant, and will not be as inclined to distract or delay you from your shamanic quest as other species of faery.

As you begin your journey into faery shamanism, remember you must build a trusting partnership with these helpful nature spirits. The creation of a faery shaman comes at the end of a long road with many potential setbacks. By focusing first on the helpful nature spirits of plants—including flowers, wildflowers, herbs, trees, shrubs, bushes, grasses, grains, and hedges—you will more easily complete the tasks within this book which should carry you through the beginner's level of faery shamanism, and leave you in an excellent position for intermediate and advanced learning at the hands of the fey themselves.

What Do They Look Like?

To be asked to describe a faery, or even a particular category of faery, is akin to being asked to describe any one of the seven billion canines currently living on our planet. It is possible to identify a category or species of faery, just as it is possible to identify a type or species of dog. Accurately identifying a fairy as belonging to a specific group is easier than identifying an individual faery within that group, just as it would be easier to identify a canine as a wolf than to isolate one wolf in a pack based on a verbal description.

Most faeries show themselves in a human-like form, although, as faery tales tell us, they often make mistakes with the full transformation. Pointy ears and shedding skin have been considered one sign of fey blood, another has been large, nocturnal eyes. Transformed faeries who seduce hapless humans are known throughout the world as well. The most common being the Siren or Lorelei of the Rhine River in Europe. Many boats attributed their floundering to a beautiful and mesmerizing faery woman who waits high atop the riverbank, singing and brushing her long lush hair as boats pass by on the Rhine below. Her siren song and her beauty were said to have lured many sailors and fishermen to their deaths on the rocky shallows of the riverbed.

Some faeries cannot transform themselves into shapes pleasing to us. These are usually not nature spirits—the faeries we wish to work with for healing—but rather they're elemental spirits of place (called genus loci) who serve a different function or those who should be avoided by humans.

It doesn't hurt to seek out what others see when looking at faery. Artist and author, Brian Froud, is a faery shaman, though he may or may not use this term in reference to himself. Take a look at his books, his oracle cards, and read what he has to say about the way faeries present themselves to him to be drawn. Not all are nature spirits, and not all are pleasant faeries. Sometimes they appear as nothing but radiating balls of light, others have faces, bodies, and human structures. Still others assume characteristics completely unfamiliar to anything we are accustomed to seeing in our earthbound world.

Appendix A provides online resources dedicated to many different organizations, artists, books, magazines, and other sites associated with the faery world. In these you will find both factual and fantasy representations of faery. Both are enchanting.

If you do all these things and are still not sure how to spot a faery, try thinking of a nature spirit, or a nature faery, as being the soul of a particular plant or tree. Now think about how you view the physical appearance of your own soul should it move slightly outside your body so it could be seen by others. This will give you an approximate idea of how plant souls may look to human eyes.

The Surprise of Faery Size

A popular Pagan author I know had never intended to work with the faeries, but his students wanted to explore this world. During a deep meditation he connected with a faery being who didn't look anything like a winged Tinkerbell from Disney World. The voice he heard was deep, booming, and seemed to reverberate endlessly. The full-throated being who appeared to him was very tall and fair—almost blinding in his beauty—with golden hair that shone like the sunshine.

Many faeries have bloodlines that date back to the times when the Old Deities were revered. The members of some of these races—the Amazons, the Valkyries, and the Tuatha de Danaan—are very large. These beings have been collectively referred to as "the ancient and shining ones," perhaps indigenous deities conquered by human immigration into their realm. Consequently, the faeries who descended from them tend to be quite tall, attractive, and attributed great powers not granted to mere mortals.

Just as there are vast differences in the physical appearances of human beings throughout the world, such it is with faery. The tiny winged faeries of the Victorian (1836–1901) and Edwardian (1901–1910) eras not only reflected the Victorians' love of flowers and gardening, but also brought faeries into an acceptable form with specific boundaries of influence on humans. This made faery a part of the need to control and conquer nature that was a basic tenet of the Victorian worldview. It also made it acceptable for Christian beliefs in faeries as the lower caste of the hierarchy of angels. To this day many Christian and New Age practitioners maintain that faeries are not just nature spirits, or the visible souls of nature, but that they are in fact the lowest order of angels. They accept that this is why these small faeries have been popular in Christendom.

Many faeries appear to us in ethnic folk costumes. Those of us who enjoy spending time in the faery realm assume that by appearing in ethnic form the faeries we see are making the contact easier for us by conveying to us their more human and familiar aspects, hence solidifying their link to humanity and to Mother Earth. This makes contact between us easier to relate to and accept as part of the natural world where our realms overlap.

What Do Faeries Sound Like?

Trying to attribute a specific sound to an individual faery, or even to a specific species of faery, is as impossible as trying to describe the character of an individual human voice. It simply cannot be done. Some speak in riddles in keeping with their playful natures. Other speak with strong, deep voices that continue to reverberate long after the sound has been made. Some speak in rhyme or in song. Some faery voices are light and high pitched, peppered with what sounds like small bells to human ears.

Still others may communicate telepathically. Their thoughts do not come to us as words, but as images flashed upon our consciousness. The pictures come and go quickly, so see as much as you can before returning a telepathic photo.

Other Identifying Characteristics

The range of faery beings covers as many individual characteristics as humans have. Since we are setting our sights on working with elemental or nature spirit faeries, there are some things to look for to tell us we are communicating with the correct beings.

Plant faeries look similar to the plants they inhabit. In a garden, faeries will look like the plant they are attached to, and will often not be able to move very far from their host plant. Those who can may offer you a gift of their energy to take back to our world to heal someone. Keep your mind open. A faery is unlikely to hand you a medical bag. You may be offered something that is ephemeral, an energy you will carry within you. Sometimes you will be offered a talisman, such as a stone or piece of jewelry.

It is true that when you return to your normal waking consciousness, your physical eyes will cease to see these gifts, although with experience you will start to see the energy patterns of things you bring back with you from the faery world.

The faery who gave you the gift, or provided instructions on how to heal, must always be thanked and given a gift in return. Coins and other shiny objects are favorite offerings.

Do not become frustrated if you are not able at first to see these gifts, feel them within you, or feel you can successfully pass the healing energy along to others. This is not a technical how-to manual. Your success comes through practice, dedication, and intuition. It is likely you will reread this book, and others on shamanism, many times before you begin to have a sense of yourself as a healer.

The Origins of the Word Faery

The term "faery" (fey, fay, fata, fate, fairy, faerie, etc.) has been attributed to many beings and many spirits. The word comes to us from the Latin fata, meaning "fate," and from the Old French word faerie, meaning "an enchantment." It has also been related to the Greco-Roman myth of the Three Fates who control the ultimate destinies of humanity. The label of faery has been applied to everything from the pre-Celtic people of Ireland and Britain, to a lower order of angels from the Judeo-Christian traditions. All have found their way into the folklore and folk beliefs of people everywhere.

Faeries have been connected with Witchcraft since before recorded history. Not only are cognates of the word "fate" still used to describe faeries in other languages, the old Romany, or Gypsy, word for faery was once the same word they used for Witch.

Faeries have been categorized into three broad classes: the helpful faeries, the harmful fairies, and the play-all-the-time faeries.

The term "faery" is braided into many cultures and theologies in the human world. Some of these titles were devised by the plain folk of Ireland, the British Isles, and Western Europe to keep the faery happy and to ward off tricks and games associated with the fey.

EUPHEMISMS FOR FAERY
The Gentle Folk
Them That Knows
The Gentry
The Genteel Ones
The Wee Ones
The Little People
The Hill Folk
The Old Ones
The House Guests
The Kindly Folk
The Seelie Court
Riders on the Wind
Knockers
The Stealthy Ones
The Tricksters
Elven Folk
Hearth People
The Fair Folk

In this book, we will concern ourselves with the subclass of faeries known as nature spirits, elementals, or divas. We will also be working with the kings and queens of the four elements—earth, air, fire, and water—that make up creation and the earth upon which we live. For our purposes we'll use the words faery and fey interchangeably.

How We Separated from Faery

One reason humans today find it difficult to connect with faery as serious partners in spiritual and physical healing is the image of faery bequeathed to us by the Victorians. Queen Victoria sat on the throne of the United Kingdom from 1837 to 1901. Her German husband, Prince Albert, possessed a strict personal moral code that frowned on things "frivolous." Theirs was the new Age of Reason, and neither the Prince, nor other moguls of science and industry, saw any end to what human-kind could achieve.

This arrogance was fed during the final push of the Industrial Revolution (roughly 1880–1912) when humans came to believe they could conquer all parts of nature and bend them to their desired roles. We thought we could force the earth to do tricks for us that it had never done before. Then as today, many people in the power seats gave little thought to the long-term consequences of their actions on human life or on the well-being of our planet.

As the Western world's emphasis shifted toward technology and materialism, nature-centered spirituality and mysticism fell out of favor. Faeries came to be portrayed as small, winged creatures who played in nature, and could sometimes play with us. They began appearing in children's storybooks, stage plays like *Peter Pan*, and in popular household adornments of the period. This was just one more way of forming nature to our appointed comfort zone, allowing us to feel we had power over—instead of power with—nature.

The folklore featuring giants, ancient races of deities, rulers of the elements, or other unmanageable creatures were consigned to the pages of storybooks and called "faerytales" as a way to put these uncontrollable features of faery in a safe place where no one had to consider their existence outside of the printed page.

The more we distanced ourselves from nature, the easier it became to treat nature as ours to do with what we willed. We lost sight of the life force within nature, and we reclassified faeries as children's nonsense.

During this same period, the Spiritualists and other believers in spirits of all types became interested in contacting the beings in otherworlds. Sadly, much trickery went on as charlatans took advantage of the gullible. Even the ever-logical Sir Arthur Conan Doyle (1859–1930), author of the Sherlock Holmes series of stories, was duped by false photos of faeries from a town in England known as Cottingley Grove (circa 1911) and wrote about them. The book, which was about two little girls who captured themselves in photos with faeries, caused controversy for years until it was proven that the "faeries" came from a children's book and the photos were fake.

This blow to believers put the acceptance of faeries as real beings on the backburner, and they would stay there for the better part of a century. As the twentieth century progressed, fewer city dwellers or those of the educated class accepted faeries as a part of their reality. In rural areas the beliefs flourished, especially as the relentless development called progress became a threat to those who lived among and respected faery.

W. Y. Evans-Wentz and Alexander Carmichael both conducted extensive interviews with rural dwellers throughout Ireland, Great Britain, and the Brittany region of France in the late nineteenth and early twentieth century. These men were two of the earliest oral historians, using a method of collecting history by talking with people who lived through specific time periods, which is a popular method of gathering history from many viewpoints in the twenty-first century.

What was discovered was that there were uncanny similarities in folk songs, work rituals, spiritual practices, and protection rites among people who lived isolated from the industrial or metropolitan areas of their home countries. Those families with names of the earliest settlers to Britain and Ireland had the most faery lore surrounding them, and they bore the responsibility to preserve it.

Some Twentieth-Century Faery Concepts

- Most often thought to be fictitious creatures
- Not part of adult reality
- Cute decorations like Cupid's silhouette
- Capricious and as likely to trick as to help
- Dangerous to the body and soul
- Could lure one to their death
- Stole children and replaced them with faery "changelings"
- Took household supplies to feed themselves
- Favored or protected homes where libations were offered
- Spoiled foods of families who did not offer them respect
- Would torment anyone who trespassed on their sacred space
- Diminutive appearance
- Human features but with flaws such as pointed ears
- Either dwarfish earth-dwellers or thin and winged fliers
- Lived in homes, barns, or natural places
- Protective of animals, wild and domestic
- Would punish someone cruel to animals
- Possessed great longevity or were immortal
- Would retaliate if they were caught in wash water or garbage

- The figure of Death was a faery
- Death could be foretold by faery behavior and song
- May 1st and Midsummer Day were when nature faeries were most active
- At Midsummer food animals had to undergo rites of protection

If Faeries Exist, Why Haven't I Seen Them?

If you're like most people, you were taught about faeries when you were very young from the storybooks your parents read to you. You probably saw cartoons and movies featuring faery beings, and Walt Disney's Tinkerbell (taken straight from the 1903 book by J. M. Barrie) became the new prototype for faeries: small, pretty, winged, but with a jealous and vengeful disposition.

Perhaps you pretended you were a faery and played games with them. Then you grew up and left the world of faery behind like an unwanted doll.

Even though you reach adulthood there are probably many things in which you believe or accept that you've never seen. You take their existence on faith alone. The most obvious example is a belief in a higher power or a creator. No one can prove this power exists, yet the vast majority of the seven billion of us on this planet accept that it exists.

Unlike a higher power, faeries live closer to our world and can be seen by the naked eye. Faeries live in a realm between the manifest world and the unseen world. They are part of the natural world, but a part which remains just out of our physical sight. This is usually referred to as "the astral world," a plane of existence which overlaps and penetrates our own, but which cannot be seen by the average adult without practice. These plant souls can become visible when we will our minds to open to their world, and occasionally we catch a glimpse of it by accident, when our minds are lulled by other thoughts.

Another reason knowledge of faeries is not made available to everyone is that the fey possess great power. World leaders, who hold the reins of power (both secular and religious) in the human sphere, can't control faery power—it lies outside their domain. Thus, it may be advantageous for them to claim certain things do not exist. Over time, subjects that have been closed to discussion are simply forgotten. Many of us recall faeries encountered in our childhood, once we are exposed again to people who believe in them and who are brave enough to relate their own childhood memories. These faeries were our playmates. We saw them because no one had told us we could not, and we enjoyed the company of our "invisible friends" until someone older—and, we thought, wiser—told us there are no such things as faeries.

To end this section, please permit me one observation: We humans are stubborn, and we often don't see anything we don't really want to see, be it something in our physical world or something more paranormal. Keep your mind open, as you did as a child, and faery will make itself known to you.

Faery Tales

When Englishman J. M. Barrie authored the popular children's story *Peter Pan* in 1903, he told us we must believe in the faeries if the faeries are to live. Such a scene-stopping intermission to beg for belief in the faery realm is not something the average Edwardian writer was inclined to do, but in the theatrical version he knew he was going to be addressing children. Barrie was also making a point about belief and of the power of the mind to shape our physical world.

Does a youthful memory beckon you back to the fey? Do you have fey blood in your ancestry? How would you describe to others what you see, feel, and experience in connection with faery? Do not just think on these questions, dream on them. For it is in the dream world, another very real place in between places, where our second sight is awakened. All we must do is let the imagery come as it will and not try to analyze it immediately. Accept what you sense or see. Discover the power of belief that you had as a child.

Why Should I Believe in Faeries?

There are many reasons to believe in faeries, but, as with any spiritual decision, it is one you must decide for yourself to accept or reject. No one else will try to persuade you, with the possible exception of faery itself. Most of us who believe in faeries were either raised with spiritual practices which did not include proselytizing, or we are part of such spiritual paths now. All we can and will tell you is, throughout the world, people of many cultures and ethnic backgrounds have believed in the existence of nature spirits, including faeries. The legends and folklore of many lands speak of mermaids, leprechauns, trolls, and other mythical beings.

If you want to exercise your cerebral side, the recorded eye-witness accounts and stories of accidental interaction with faery are well substantiated. Scottish writer and philosopher, Thomas the Rhymer, and Scottish clergyman, Rev. Robert Kirk, both vanished for many years. When they reappeared they looked not a day older, and both related similar experiences inside the faery realm. W. Y. Evans-Wentz collected enchanting faery lore in the early twentieth century. His book, *Fairy Faith in Celtic Countries*, is a classic in its genre and has remained in print almost continually since it was first published in 1911.

These stories are more than the musings of uneducated, rural people who lived more than a century ago. These beliefs remain strong in many Celtic countries today. In the late twentieth century the international airport at Shannon, Ireland, needed to create longer, wider runways to accommodate larger airplanes. As the construction progressed on one of these runways, the Irish work crew realized they would have to destroy a hawthorn tree, a bush sacred to faeries. Not one worker could be persuaded to continue the work, and no one in the country could be found willing to move or remove the small tree. The work crews would not return to the job even if someone else moved the tree. Construction stopped and Shannon rerouted its proposed runway.

Faeries can teach us how to care for nature and the earth. They can assist us in healing and other endeavors that require a spiritual energy beyond what we humans can raise alone within ourselves. This is always true if you believe in them, make positive contact, and work together with mutual respect.

Faeries and Religion

It's not necessary to espouse any particular religion or spiritual path to make a connection with the spirits of the earth, any more than you have to espouse a particular religion to engage in meaningful relationships with your pets. You need only recognize that these beings are our equals, made by the same creator, put here for a purpose, and deserving of the respect we give to any deity-given life form.

The word religion comes from a Greek word meaning "to relink." Today Pagans, Wiccans, and other followers of earth-honoring religions, as well as New Age seekers from all spiritual backgrounds, are attempting to relink or reclaim partnership with the fey. We are changing our thinking about the many worlds our spirits can traverse. We are learning to listen to nature with our hearts and minds rather than our ears, and to form a closer bond with all the earth's residents. We seek to have power *with* rather than power *over* others.

Faeries are not worshiped today as deities, though many have their roots in very old Pagan deities. One of the easiest ways to end the worship of the old deities was to diabolize them, turning them into dangerous legions of an Antigod they created and named Satan. Look into paintings of faery. Notice the pointed ear, the large nocturnal eyes, and you will see the vestiges of this demonizing of faery. Today they represent an Antigod from Jewish biblical texts who was never meant to be personified.

2
Answering the Call to Become a Faery Shaman

Since the early 1990s, we've seen an explosion of books, magazines, clothing, music, artwork, etc., that honor the nature spirits. Visit any New Age store and you'll see myriad faery images on everything from jewelry to candles. Search the Internet and you'll find many thousands of websites devoted to the faery.

By answering the call to become a faery shaman you will be helping to keep the light inside the faery kingdom shining like a beacon for those wise ones who follow you. You will be part of the movement of humans and faeries who have set the goal to reverse the decree of MacLir and to avoid self-destruction. Your knowledge and experience will help others to see the truth about the fey.

Our mutual creator already connects us with faery, we need only open ourselves in respectful cooperation. To accept that nature has much to teach us about ourselves is to recognize the connection of all life. If you answer the call to be a faery shaman you will join those who walk with a foot in both worlds, seeking partnership and healing for body, mind, spirit, and our earth. The chapters that follow will explain the process of becoming a faery shaman.

Listen to the faeries calling, and, if you are up to the challenge, answer their plea.

It's a Lifetime Commitment

Shamans who have interacted with faeries will to tell you that when you forge these bonds of cooperation, it's a lifetime commitment. Once you pledge yourself to a common goal with faery, you will not be permitted to change your mind or shuffle halfheartedly along the path.

Like any path, the path of the faery shaman has its rewards and frustrations. Be sure you are up to the task before embarking on this venture. If you have any doubts, turn back and wait for them to invite you again.

To regain a working partnership with the fey you must first overcome the brainwashing that separated us from faery in the first place. You must be willing to start tearing a hole in the cloak that divides our worlds. Two species. Two realms. One place in common: Mother Earth.

Not everyone who interacts with faery wants or needs to undertake the task of becoming a faery shaman. Many people enjoy a daily relationship with the fey without making this commitment.

The fey enjoy play. Dancing, feasting, riding, drinking, and music are their weaknesses, and they welcome accepting humans into their revels. The only caution is to be very aware of what you accept from them and how long you stay with them.

Time does not exist outside of our known universe, at least that's what the physicists tell us. Faery is not our universe, and time can seem to pass very quickly or slowly in their world. If you don't try to keep track of time for yourself, the faeries will not. They have no use for time and their lives are not regimented to a clock.

Much folklore talks about the dangers of accepting food and drink from faery hands in the belief that this will entrap them inside the faery realm until the fey wish to release them. I once adhered to this precaution, but I have since relaxed my practice. Celtic society, from which much of our western faery lore derives, placed the obligations of hospitality high on their code of honor. Irish folklore is littered with stories of clans who entertained their enemies while under the obligation—called a geis (pronounced as one syllable, gay-shh)—of the rules of hospitality. There are also wicked stories about what happened to those who took advantage of this practice.

The Earliest Calling

Like me, many people first interacted with the fey in childhood. We now recognize our experiences of faeries were not dreams or imaginary playmates. I have heard from hundreds of people who have shared experiences similar to mine. We can't all be "seeing things," and we're not subject to mass hysteria. No matter what science and "rational people" may tell us, those of us who were permitted to share the beauty of faery at a young age will never stop believing.

The fey are often visible to children. But children's reports are dismissed by adults as an overactive imagination, the childish creation of "invisible friends," and nothing more substantial. As children reach their school years, those memories of the encounters with faery fade, and remain buried in the subconscious until something they read or see in adulthood jogs those memories.

The Healing Power of Faery contains many personal stories of encounters with the fey. Some are from my own experience. Others were told to me in faery-related workshops, at spiritual gatherings or events. These stories were shared with me for the purpose of helping others to pinpoint a moment in time when they were "pixy-led," or called by the fey to work in partnership. Not all encounters are pleasant—some of the fey can be as unpredictable as the winds on which they ride—but all of them have something to teach us.

Today, we recognize that we were called by faery many times before to join in active work with the awesome powers of nature. Many people have been called. Many have answered. Many more do not recognize the call, or fear it because it seems opposed to all they've been taught since their own childhood. No one said change is easy, but change is vital in many arenas if life is to continue on this planet.

Faery Tales

Many cultures believe that fey children are occasionally born to a human couple. They are babies born of a human lineage that mixed with faery blood in the deep past. These children often possess keen psychic abilities or healing gifts. Sometimes they are born with a caul (a thin membrane covering the head) over their faces—some even have pointed ears.

By putting out a welcoming hand, believing in the power of this partnership, we can turn healing energy into a dynamic force, a tidal wave of healing that can blanket our earth and all who depend on her. Connecting to faery in a meaningful and mutually helpful way takes more than recognition of one another's existence, however. It also takes effort and patience.

What You Can Bring the Faeries

The fey want only three things from us: validation, respect, and help in preserving the world of nature upon which they are symbiotically dependent for their lives between the astral world and our physical world. When you consider all they are willing to give to us if only we make a polite effort, their desires are not extravagant.

Validation simply means they wish to be recognized again as a real race of beings, as diverse and unique as the human race. You need not know every detail about the fey, or even about one specific type of faery, but they do demand you accept them as they are and for what they are. We ask the same of them, do we not?

Respect? This is not a difficult concept to grasp, though many people have big problems being respectful every day with everyone they encounter. Rudeness accomplishes nothing, and it might even hinder your efforts. This is why there were no answers to the basic questions of who, what, where, when, or how? Each faery species is unique, and so is each individual faery. Everyone knows that the words, "They all look alike to me," is offensive and degrading. You wouldn't, I hope, say this to another person, so why would you say it in the presence of any other sentient being? Fey feelings are sensitive, as they should be in this case, so remember to be understanding and respectful at all times. The last thing they ask of us is the most difficult. We are all aware of the harm that has been done to the earth's ecosystems. They have been polluted, and destroyed, and otherwise uncared for. It is inevitable that those ecosystems that aren't already extinct, soon will be. We must be ever mindful of how we treat the earth. While we have been making strides in becoming "green," we can still do much, much more to save natural resources and energy. Keep in mind that this not only preserves the faeries' homes, but ours as well.

3

Games Faery Play

Faeries know how to play as well as how to be serious. They can teach us to slow down and make time for fun. The inhabitants of the faery realm enjoy games, tests, and other sport with those of us seeking entrance into their world. Everyone who approaches faery will have to deal with mind games. Some of this comes from the nature spirits' naturally playful personalities. It also helps them to determine if we are worthy of partnership with them. The fey learn to trust us by testing us; they challenge us by working and playing with rules that are unfamiliar to us.

The ups and downs of connecting with faery comprise some of the most amusing stories in the metaphysical world, but these tales aren't often shared with others. Even some faery games that are not funny at the time get great laughs in retrospect. Here's an example.

I once knew a young man with long hair who drove a shiny red sports car. At least once a week he was pulled over by a law enforcement official because he fit the profile of a reckless youthful driver. However, this man never speeded and was very cautious when driving.

This man was also trying to develop a working relationship with faery, but he was much too arrogant in his approach. One day as he drove home from work he was stopped by the Texas State Police and asked for his driver's license. He flipped his wallet open, certain that his license would be there as it always was. To his surprise the license was missing. He knew he hadn't removed it from his wallet and felt a wave of panic. The patrolman called in the license plate and learned the young man had no record of moving violations and that he did indeed have a valid driver's license. The officer let him go.

Feeling shaken and confused, the young man went home to search for his driver's license. He found it sitting on his dresser in plain view. Someone had taken it from his wallet and placed it on the dresser, but it wasn't him. He knew the culprits were the fey. The incident reminded him that he needed to make an attitude adjustment if he wished to avoid further adventures with the State Police.

Pixy-Led

Some fey want nothing more than playmates. Others are testing your temperament to see if you can laugh at yourself. They want to know if you're relaxed enough to partner with them in their work.

Many races of astral beings comprise faery, and not all are the nature spirits with whom we can work with in healing. Some races of faery want to distract us. A few of the faery dislike humans and hope to harm us, or at least put us on a path that leads nowhere. We often call this game of hide and chase being "pixy-led." The various denizens of faery lead us into a world with rules and customs so different from ours that we wonder at first how any productive partnership can ever be forged.

These encounters can be scary, or they can seem to be a waste of time. Even the faery who are looking for a serious magickal partnership with us can be difficult: they may seem easily offended or capricious. I am acquainted with several seekers who, during their years of working and playing with the fey, have had their world shaken up a few times when faery wanted their attention.

A woman friend of mine has been involved with nature spirituality for more than a decade. She worked to form strong, happy bonds with the faery, who have been visible to her since childhood. But even after all this time together, she found they are not shy about making their displeasure known should she do something they find annoying or inconsiderate.

Her two house cats are often seen playing with invisible beings. When she took the cats to the vet for annual checkups, she removed their collars to which she'd attached jingle bells. But she forgot to put the collars back on the cats when they returned home. Soon some very strange things began happening in her house. The television turned itself on and off, items would go missing only to turn up in their usual places a few hours later. Little voices startled visitors.

The longer this went on, the stronger the phenomena became, until my friend was getting up several times at night to turn off lights, appliances, and other things that seemed to have minds of their own. Finally, she figured out the problem. The faeries wanted the bells put back on the cats. Cats are not their favorite animals in the first place, and having two playful ones sneak up on the faeries without warning was not just inconvenient, but dangerous. My friend put the belled collars back on her cats and her house settled once again into a peaceful refuge for her and her fey friends.

Faery Etiquette

If you happen to see a small person walking about your house minding his or her own business, there's no need to attack him or her. Granted, the sudden appearance of a faery can be startling. Try to remain relaxed, however, and take it all in stride. Tormenting the little guy will only bring the wrath of faery down on your house, and you will be very, very sorry before they accept your apology.

When approaching faery accept that these beings are individuals. Some are nature spirits living between the closest planes of the natural world and our world. They may belong to what we would call subclasses of the faery world, but they are sentient beings with free will. They are not beneath us on the scale of spiritual evolution, to be ordered about by us. Most of the others, however, are vestiges of powerful deities or genus loci, Latin for "spirits of place." Offending them is never wise.

Human beings mean well when attempting to connect with faery, but we are also an arrogant race of beings. Even those of us whose spiritual paths lead us into the deepest reaches of Mother Earth make mistakes.

A friend of mine decided to use faery as his personal wishing well and began making demands for things he wanted rather than needed.

The offerings he gave to the fey in return were far below the value of the services for which he was asking. Worse still, he never asked faery what he could do for them in exchange.

Soon objects he owned began disappearing or got broken. At the same time, his desire for material things spun out of control. When he finally connected the bad luck with the fey his objects returned. Today this man respects faery and its power. He maintains a lovely faery shrine in his yard, hidden from view by tall trees, which vibrates with positive spiritual energy.

Do's and Don'ts of Faery Interaction

The world of faery has its own code of rules and hospitality. Though these rules can appear anarchic to modern humans, there is order in what we may consider chaos. The fey expect us to learn their rules and bend from our familiar human customs of behavior while in their world.

The first rule of partnership is that no one gives commands to anyone for any reason. We and faery are equal in terms of free will. Neither of us likes having orders shouted at us, or demands made that take time and energy away from the higher good our partnership is supposed to produce. We have to start respecting one another for what we are, not what we wish the other to be.

The following is a list of appropriate and inappropriate actions when trying to build a relationship with faery.

- Do refer to faeries with respect.
- Do see yourself and them as equals in every way.
- Do give offerings of value.
- Do give more than you take.
- Do offer them food or drink.
- Do set up a shrine or altar for the faeries.
- Do invite them in from the cold. Only snow and ice faeries, led by old Jack Frost, want to be out in the cold weather. Some woodland faeries hibernate with the animals.
- Do watch for faeries before you throw things from your house to the yard or curb.

- Don't speak to them in childish gibberish.
- Don't assume faeries are stupid.
- Don't underestimate the power of faery to turn your world upside down and inside out.
- Don't assume faeries are not present, even when you cannot see them.
- Don't presume faeries will or should just go away peacefully.
- Don't expect them to be your psychic shield.
- Don't allow pets to run free without warning the fey, especially cats.
- Don't underestimate their hurt feelings.
- Don't issue commands to these beings.
- Don't demand faeries answer the riddles they give you.
- Don't move a shrine or altar without asking permission.
- Don't go back on your word. In spite of a love of word games, the fey are not liars and do not tolerate lies no matter the reason.
- Don't take back a gift you've given to the faeries.
- Don't cut plants without the faery of that plant's permission.
- Don't gossip with malicious intent.
- Don't harm an animal unless you are using it to feed your family, and always be respectful of that animal's sacrifice.
- Don't ask a faery to assist you in any work that might bring harm to others.
- Don't enter a wooded area that may be sacred to the faeries without permission and appropriate offerings.
- Don't treat the fey, no matter how cute one might be, like children.

Common sense dictates most of our interactions with other people, why should it not be the same for faery? If you're still thinking these beings are somehow our inferiors, it's time to drop out of the faery shaman quest. The fey are different, that's all. Being different does not imply a value judgment.

Learning about the Astral World

Before you leap into guided meditations and begin your shaman quest, you need to spend some time learning about the astral world, its rules, and how to safely enter and exit this realm.

In my previous book, *Astral Projection for Beginners* (Llewellyn, 1997), I presented six different techniques to practice astral projection. The most important thing to remember is to let go of your preconceived ideas about the astral world, faeries, and otherworld landscapes and allow your experience to be unique. Trust in it. Trust in yourself.

Also, everyone's mind is capable of reaching into otherworlds. A daydream is an example of being on the edge of the astral plane. Your body is in one place, but your conscious mind is in another, and, for that time, you are elsewhere.

Spend some time in the quiet. Get comfortable. Uncross legs and arms. Breathe deeply and envision unwanted thoughts flowing out of you until you feel a sort of cleansing has occurred. This is often referred to as finding your center. When you feel fully relaxed try to put your conscious mind somewhere nearby, but away from your physical body. Imagine it seeing the room or landscape from the perspective of your mind, just as if it had taken your eyes with it when it left you. You will find at first that it is difficult to keep your mind focused on your goal. This is natural. When it happens do not get frustrated and give up, simply bring your consciousness back where you want it to be.

This projecting of one's consciousness is something that is learned and perfected with time. It's not an easy task. Everyday our brains are on overload with information blasting us from the workplace, the traffic, music, television, telephones, etc. Quiet time is almost an oxymoron. These are all reasons to try harder, not excuses to allow you to fail. A shaman must be able to maintain a consciousness in another world to do his or her job. Start practicing as soon as possible, and keep practicing until you become adept at this art.

4

Building a Friendship with Faeries

Nature spirits are as real as you or me. They simply live on a plane of existence slightly removed from ours. When they try, they can see us, so why would we not be able to see them? The only reason they see us with greater ease is that no one has taught them, "There are no such things as people." The faery mind remains open to the possibilities of all separate worlds even though they continue to live primarily in one.

Are You Really, Really Ready to Be a Faery Shaman?

Are you ready to be a faery shaman? Think carefully. If you step onto the path of the faery shaman, you will be on it for the rest of this lifetime. *The Healing Power of Faery* is a guide to becoming a faery shaman, someone who traverses the rim of the world of humans and the world of nature as if no boundaries exist between the two. The gift is also a glorious version of second sight. Most of the world of faery is beautiful and entrancing enough that many who find their way to this semihidden world—shaman or not—do not wish to leave.

A faery shaman performs serious duties. Once committed, you cannot turn back. Lives and spirits are at stake, and the fey will count on you for your help. Take this little quiz to see if you are up to the task.

1. Are you the kind of person who would get out of a warm bed in the middle of the night to help a friend?
2. How well have you honored commitments you have made to others in the past? Have you taken good care of your pets for the entire span of their lives? How about your children? Other friends and relatives?
3. Are you empathetic? If so, how do you handle the emotional pain you witness in others?
4. Do you tend to judge others before you know their stories?
5. Do you show active compassion for creatures smaller and weaker than you?
6. Are you willing to be on call every moment of every day if you are summoned to help someone, human or not?
7. Do you have the patience to work with faery? To listen to their advice, go in and out of their world, to deal with their tricksters, and to play their games and riddles?
8. Is helping someone needing to be healed important to you?
9. Can you give up the need to always be right?

Faeries will often appear to you in the physical world when you least expect them. In many ways they are like ghosts—they do not perform on command. When you're running all the recording equipment they stay away, only to put on a spectacular show once the cameras are turned off. Meeting them does require a calm spirit and patience. If you feel the need to take a boom box everywhere you go, the fey will stay away.

You can see faeries with your normal vision, as well as in an astral projection state where your consciousness is separated from your body. It might even be fair to say that the fey play hard to get. Who can blame them?

Must you see something to accept its existence? Think about this carefully. Do you believe in a creator or a god you cannot see? Do you accept that you have the love of a parent or close friend? Do you believe in a heaven, hell, or other afterlife world? There are many things, entities, and places we accept on faith without expecting empirical proof of their existence.

Because faery inhabits a plane of existence that bridges the seen and the unseen worlds, you will have to practice using indirect sight to see them in the physical. Begin training your eyes to do this by gazing at a large portrait or painting of people involved in something that involves motion. I use a print of ballroom dancers poised to begin moving around the ballroom. Don't look at these figures, look through them. Lock your gaze just before the image begins to double. Lock it there and, with your indirect sight, wait for the optical illusion to begin, the one that gives movement to the still life.

Once you've developed your talent in this venue, take yourself into a natural and safe spot with lots of plants, wildflowers, and trees. Select one that is most pleasing to you and try the same technique. Because faeries are not inanimate objects as your picture was, but sentient beings, their movement will at first surprise you. Their movements will be more defined. This may jolt you from your concentration, and that's just fine. Try again and you will soon see the faery of the plant moving around and making sounds or gestures to you. Most of these nature spirits cannot go too far from their physical world hosts, but may surprise you with what they can do in a small space.

Over time you will learn to fall into this special sight at will, and your adventures in faery will be easier and more fulfilling.

Faery Tales

For centuries, we've believed that faeries own a huge cauldron of gold at the end of the rainbow, and whoever captures its guardian will have all the wealth of the cauldron. The cauldron, however, is not a receptacle of earthly wealth, but of spiritual riches. In the iconography of most civilizations, the cauldron, chalice, or bowl is symbolic of the womb of Mother Earth or another mother deity.

Making Your Home Welcoming to Faeries

A warm hearth is a metaphor for a place that was once very real in virtually every dwelling place on earth. This hearth is not just the fireplace, but the kitchen, the furnace, the stove, and the space heater. A "warm hearth" is any warmth you provide for your faery friends. Even a pretty arrangement of candles will work if you state aloud that you are inviting your faery friends to live there.

Another way you can show faeries they are welcome at the hearth is by offering them libations. You'll find copious folklore available concerning their preferences. Among these are milk, butter, and whiskey. Don't just give them your leftovers. If you want to befriend the fey you must give them your best, as you would any honored guest.

Popular Libations and Gifts for Faeries

- Milk
- Cream
- Whiskey
- Wine
- Honey
- Bread
- Butter
- Meade
- Ale
- Silver
- Shiny objects
- Special stones
- New coins
- Drinking gourd
- Chalice
- Small figurines
- Bells

Creating Your Faery Altar or Shrine

One thing you can do to show your devotion and commitment to this path is to set up a permanent altar or shrine to the faeries. This can be as large or small as you want or need it to be. What is important is your perpetual care of this sacred space. By creating it you are saying to the universe that you wish to serve and honor faery. Both faery and the universe will expect you to make good on your promise. This means keeping it clean, updating and refreshing it in accordance with the seasons, and making offerings.

There are no etched-in-stone differences between an altar and a shrine. Both are places for meeting between the worlds, for communicating needs and emotions, and to honor the faeries who choose to accept you as a partner in shamanic healing. They also provide faery a place of focus, where they can feel safe in your world. This is where they can visit you privately, and where you can give them gifts and other offerings.

Where and When to Erect It

Shrines and altars can be erected inside or outdoors, or even combined with other altars or shrines as long as the area set aside for faery is clearly demarcated. Ideally, we would all like to be walking across our own land, or through a verdant forest, and just stumble across a faery shrine to adopt. These places still exist in nature and serve as the homes and the shrine of faery—if you're lucky, you might discover one.

An outdoor shrine should be in a spot where neighbors are not likely to see it or walk through it. If you have a garden on your property, this is an ideal space to put a shrine. Everything you need is already there except the offering bowl. Another perfect location for an altar or shrine is in a clearing sheltered by bushes and trees. These are nature faery homes, and making their living place even nicer will endear you to the faeries.

House faeries, like the Brownies of Scotland and the Lares of old Rome, prefer to have their gifts presented indoors. A fireplace is the ideal spot because it has traditionally been the heart of the home. The modern hearth is the kitchen, and food libations are often presented in this room. Be certain your pets or children can't get to these for both safety and spiritual reasons.

If you have a nice basement well sealed against unwanted pests, this also makes a good place for an altar or shrine. Attics also work, as do window gardens. I have used the top of my dresser and an occasional table built by my great-grandfather as places to honor faery.

My experience and observations tell me that it is best to begin to erect the altar or shrine early in your introduction into the faery kingdom. This shows you are serious about your intent to become a faery shaman. When you've been initiated as a faery shaman, the altar or shrine is where you'll welcome faery into your environment.

What You'll Need

Your faery shrine should contain three primary things:

1. A place to make faery offerings of coins, stones, etc.;
2. A representation of one of the four elements for faeries to rest upon: a stone, bowl of water, or candle, for example;
3. A representation of the faeries themselves, such as plants that belong to them, scents they favor, statues, or paintings.

After these elements are in place, you can get creative. Flowering plants are favorites of faeries, so you'll probably want to keep a plant or two on your altar for them. On my altar I have a plant in which I hide shiny objects for the faeries. I also have a crescent moon looking glass. Faeries love the shine of glass and are known to become enraptured with their own reflections. If your shrine is outdoors you might include a large statue, perhaps one with solar collectors to light it at night.

Scent seems to run a close second to flowering plants for attracting faeries. Place a tea light candle inside a small cauldron and set it on a fire-proof kitchen tile or trivet. Around the candle use a little bit of essential oil. Keep the scent light and use very little oil. The lit candle warms the oil and scents the room. Tea lights also have a short burning life, so you can be present to monitor the fire and enjoy the faeries it attracts.

Be as creative as you dare. There are so many things to choose from: art prints, wall tiles, photographs, statuettes, flowers, posters, stickers . . . the fey welcome them all. Make sure you, too, like the setup or decor of this sacred space—you may be spending a lot of time here.

Don't think just because you're "done for now" that your altar or shrine is complete. As your partnership develops, you will find gifts from the fey, new knickknacks, and astounding artwork you'll want to add. Let this sacred space grow as your relationship with faery grows. Don't be surprised if it goes through dramatic changes over time, as you and faery grow together, and as your mutual needs change.

Inviting Faeries to Your Shrine

When you have constructed your shrine to a degree that it is worthy of inviting in faery—it does not have to be completed—simply make them an offering of coin or stone, and a libation of milk, bread, honey, or whiskey. Tell the faeries out loud that you have created this sacred space for them to work, play, and rest.

Let faery know they will be honored here and that no harm shall come to them, and then be prepared to follow through on that promise. This means you must be careful with cleaning products and yard chemicals. Make sure pets and children will not destroy the shrine or use it as a toy.

What you say when inviting the faeries in is far less important than the sincerity behind your words. A faery can pick out a con job quicker than any vice squad. If you don't know where to start, try something such as:

> To home to hearth, to field and tree,
> To all the Good Gentry I say, "Blesséd Be";
> Gifts and token you shall be given,
> All evil energy from here is driven;
> In works of healing and health I do,
> Request the assistance of all of you.
> I open this altar/shine to honor your fame,
> And I will give you my secret name.
> So on one another we may depend,
> And so must it be from now 'til time's end.

Your announcement that your shrine or altar is open for business need not be in rhyme. I prefer to use rhyming when possible because it helps me remember the words. There is a feeling of empowerment in reciting words you know by heart. You can put your energy into your meaning rather than worrying about reading a script. You cannot go wrong either way, however, for the fey won't be offended by a written script. Again, that these words come from your heart and are sincerely meant are what's most important.

Sample Ideas for Your Shrine

Still not sure? Here are some suggestions from my own shrines and the shrines and altars of my friends. Choose the ones that will increase your enjoyment of the sacred space you create.

- Put faery prints, tiles, or artwork on the walls. See Appendix A for help in finding these, or contact your local metaphysical store.
- Use photos from magazines and attach them with double-sided cellophane tape.
- Use live nontoxic plants and flowers in and around your house to attract positive faery energy.
- Never harm a living plant or tree either outside or within the shrine area, and that means no nails in the trees; ribbons tied loosely with lots of room for the branch to expand are better.
- Use only biodegradable products with your outside offerings of food; neither the fey nor the area wildlife have any use for plastic.
- Hang sparkly items on trees and bushes; faery loves shiny objects.
- If you have an area where it is safe to hang glass, put up a mirror. Faeries are enraptured by their own reflections.
- Wind chimes are fun, and the fey like them shiny, but be cautious about the timbre of the chimes. Some species of faeries are frightened away by bells.
- String shiny baubles around the area; this creates a festive look that both humans and faery can enjoy.
- Sprinkle faery dust—available at occult stores or from online dealers—over the area.
- For illumination, string up solar-powered strands of lights.
- Invite faery to your shrine area by creating enticing resting spots, such as large toadstools or soft beds of sweet grasses (but not if children or pets have access to the shrine or altar as many of these plants are toxic).
- Plant flowers and herbs the faeries love most; among these are primrose, lilac, lavender, pussywillows, honesty, honeysuckle, mugwort, white sage, gardenia, moonwort, mullein, cattails, lilies, lily of the valley, elder trees, hawthorn, oleander, and sweet pea. Some of these are strong poisons, particularly the lily of the valley and the oleander. Consider your own and your neighbors' children or animals before planting. Do your research too. A standard field guide to herbs or to magickal

herbs can be found in most bookstores, and information is also available online. Do your research but, when in doubt, err on the side of caution.

- Place offerings or shrines at the bases of trees the fey are known to love, which include willow, holly, hawthorn, elder, rowan, birch, apple, banyan, and coconut palms.
- Many wildflowers are also favorite living quarters for plant spirits, and include Queen Anne's lace, goldenrod, bachelor buttons, mullein, mugwort, purselane, and ragweed.
- Use items made of glass only if you are certain they will not topple and break, or present a danger to children and animals who visit the area.
- Purchase figurines or statuettes of faeries and give them permanent homes on your altar or shrine. These are available in New Age stores, home decor shops, and online—your biggest problem will be narrowing down the selections.
- Hang colorful eggs around the shrine in spring.
- Use white and glitter decorations for the winter faeries and old Jack Frost.
- Offer wildflowers, mistletoe, and early grains in the summertime, being cautious about what you put out if children or pets can access your altar or shrine area.
- Gather leaves or tree foliage in spring and summer for your altar, and brightly colored fallen leaves in autumn.
- Hang ribbons on a wreath of dried vine and keep it in the faery shrine. Add to it as needed, choosing colors that seem appropriate.
- Hang a wreath of wood on a friendly tree and tie ribbons or strips of cloth on it to represent a healing need, or as a decoration to honor the faery spirits. Invite others who cherish the fey to do the same and you will make a potent healing talisman.
- Dedicate an art or craft project as a symbol of welcome.
- Make or place a small faery house for the fey to call their own. You can put one inside, outside, or both.
- When there are no safety concerns, allow children to play at the altar. Faeries and children are natural playmates.

- Keep cats away from the shrine or altar unless you have an unusual cat who enjoys playing with the fey, rather than trying to catch them for dinner.
- Most dogs become very protective of faery shrines, but keep an eye on your pets during the first few weeks your faery altar, house, or shrine is erected to make sure they are honoring, protecting, or enjoying their time with the fey.
- Hang fresh or dried flowers or corn shucks on the altar, depending on the season.
- Apples, berries, and dried foliage make beautiful autumn decorations for an altar or shrine. Many cultures hold apples in high regard, as they were once sacred to deities of the past.
- Shiny beads, buttons, stones, coins, and other baubles are much appreciated by the fey, but avoid lavish sprinklings of glitter or faery dust—the fey can make their own quite well. Again, be conscious of children or pets. Small, shiny objects can be attractive, but they can also cause choking.

Faery Alert

Do not become frustrated with slow responses from faery. Move-in day may not happen immediately. Because faeries are living beings, they go through the same emotional ups and downs we do, and experience biorhythm cycles during which their energies ebb and rise, just as ours do.

As you build your altar or shrine new ideas will come to you. Knick-knacks lying around your house that you don't know why you're keeping may suddenly take on new meaning. Be willing to experiment. If it doesn't work for you, or if the fey make it clear they do not like what you've done, you can always take it down and rebuild using your new perceptions from the world of faery.

Starting a Friendship with Faeries

Now it is time to reach out the hand of friendship, something you must do before you enter the guided meditation in which you will declare yourself a faery shaman initiate. How do we know when we're reaching out to faery and that the gesture is being acknowledged? In the same way you would determine the success of any new acquaintance. When you shake someone's hand or give a friend a hug, that person's gestures and body postures provide nonverbal clues to his/her feelings about you. The same holds true when you meet faeries. If this is a positive meeting, then positive experiences will reinforce it. You might see butterflies, fireflies, or other animal life you normally do not see. You may feel a cool breeze if it's a hot day, or a warm beacon of sun peeking through rain clouds.

Your own mood is another good indicator of how well your initial efforts of faery friendship are going. If you feel very sad or uncomfortable, your overtures are either not welcome, or you need to try to make contact elsewhere. If you feel lighthearted, or if you giggle, then you can be sure your friendship has been accepted by the faeries.

Where to Find Faeries

Once again, this is a question that has no clear or definite answer. The faeries we know as nature or plant spirits do not live in a part of our world that is easy to see. If it was easy, everyone would be doing it and this book would be unnecessary. It is possible to see faeries on our earth plane just as they see us here, but it takes practice, and often times it takes the trust of a faery who wants to present itself to you. When you are out in nature try using your "soft sight," a drowsy state in which you look past or through what you want to see rather than fix your eyes on it directly. You may notice them just outside your normal range of vision. Do not get discouraged if you don't achieve satisfactory results the first time you try—seeking the fey may take a little time and persistence.

Sometimes it is easier to get acquainted on the astral level first; going to their home instead. Some would-be faery shamans like astral work because they don't "have to do much." Laziness is a trait faery cannot tolerate. Reading children's fairy tales will convince you of that much. Even if you are doing well with the faeries in the astral plane, they may decide it is time for you to seek them in nature. You could begin in your backyard or a local park. Until a bond of some kind is forged, you are not going to find faeries just popping into your living room to say hello, and the fey will grow tired of always meeting on your terms.

The faery like caves, seashores, trees, meadows, and natural grottos in forests. Celtic faery mythology teaches us that the places and times that are best for magickal workings are those that fall "in between." Where does seashore stop and ocean begin? Where are you neither totally in or out of the cave? When is it not quite day, but not yet night? Where do garden and prairie demarcate? Offering libations in these in-between places may hasten the faery desire to know you better because you've obviously bothered to learn something about them.

Pagans have been aware for at least 3,000 years that European faeries were most active during our solar festivals, or eight annual sabbats, particularly Ostara, Beltane, and Midsummer. Ostara comes at the time of the vernal equinox, Beltane around May 1, and Midsummer (also known as Litha) at the summer solstice. In the southern hemisphere the seasons are reversed, so look for faeries on Mabon, Samhain, and Midwinter respectively. Your chances of encountering playful faeries are best on these nights and throughout the three months these festival dates cover.

Faery Tales

William Shakespeare capitalized on the mystery of Midsummer's night to create one of his most enchanting plays. *A Midsummer Night's Dream*, in which faeries play major roles, delights us today as much as it did seventeenth-century audiences.

How to Approach a Faery

The answer to this question depends on three factors:

1. Your desire to partner with the fey for your mutual benefit
2. A faery who wants to reach you for mutual benefit
3. The type of faery you are contacting

In the world of nature spirits you will find most to be friendly, helpful, and excessively playful. There are other faeries who prefer the old ways of separation, and they do not want to reconnect with humanity. These will be easy to spot because they won't be attached to a plant and they won't banter back and forth, feeling you out as a possible working partner.

Good manners, sincerity, and acceptance of these beings as your equals smooths the connection process. Oftentimes it is best just to let the faery do and say what it likes as you get to know one another, taking your cues about words and actions from the faery itself.

The better question is, how can you make the strongest possible connection with these beings who live between our world and the etheric plane at the edge of nature? Approach them as you would anyone else you wanted to know better, especially if that person is from a culture different from yours, with customs, codes of politeness, and social behavior foreign to you. Making an effort to understand and interact with people whose daily routines are foreign to you requires special effort. The same is true for approaching faery—but it's worth the effort.

Protecting Yourself from Faery Tricks and Diversions

No matter how strong your bonds are with nature spirits and the spirits of the elements, there are other species of faery who do not like humans—they never did, and they will put a lot of effort into diverting you from your path. As stated before, animosity and mistrust have grown up over the years between our races. However, not all faeries who try to divert you are malicious. Some, such as dryads or tree spirits, are quite friendly—they're just too playful and their games can throw you off track.

To guard against this, you can use some of the old folkloric protections against faeries. These protections tend to block the faeries who bear humans ill will, and seem not to deter the faeries who want to be in our lives. Before you venture off into the woods, the astral plane, or your garden in search of faeries, read the following methods of protection and enact one or two.

- Turn your coat pockets out.
- Spin around three times counterclockwise before entering your home.

- Carry a piece of iron with you at all times. Place bits of scrap iron around your house, or keep an iron nail in your right front pocket.
- Watch where you throw waste paper or water in case you douse the fey in the process.
- Hang farm tools such as scythes carefully and securely over doorways.
- Leave your broom lying across your chimney opening or by your stove overnight.
- Nail horseshoes over doorways with the open ends up.
- Use wind chimes or door harps to frighten spirits away.
- Burn incense or sage—faeries are said to hate smoke of any kind.
- Place miniature mirrors outside your home; faeries can spend many happy hours gazing at their reflections.
- Tie up twigs from an oak, an ash, and a thorn tree (ask permission from the trees first) and place the bundle over the main entrance to your home.
- The English believe that gorse hedges, rue, and heather will keep faeries away.
- Carry a packet of sea salt in your pocket or purse, preferably on the right side of your body.
- Ring bells or make other sudden and loud noises; faery ears are sensitive and they will move on if an environment is too noisy.
- Wear daisy chains, just like the ones you made as a child.
- Put some of the herb mothan in a faery libation of milk to send them away without harming them.
- A hot coal in your butter churn will keep faeries from stealing it. (I know that one had you really worried!)

Now that you've demonstrated your willingness to establish this partnership, it is time to embark on the final preparations necessary for you to enter the world of faery and come out a new faery shaman.

Remember, there is no shame in turning back, and great courage is attributed to those who try a second time, after they have done more research and feel up to the task. Also, not everyone has to be a shaman to enjoy the faery world. You can make friends with the fey without any healing energies being exchanged. The fey are susceptible to a host of illnesses, many of them unknown to us, and may tell you you need to see a doctor, but if their type of healing is not part of your agenda, the fey will not push it upon you.

5

Becoming Initiated as a Faery Shaman

The landscape of faery is different for everyone. As is true of any collection of archetypes, there are also surprising similarities in the journeys humans undertake in the faery realm. One of the most interesting aspects of guided meditation for me is listening to a group compare experiences, sights, scents, landscapes, and other similarities when the process is over. Many have unique experiences, and I am usually fortunate enough to have a few special people share those with me. They are always enlightening. Often the seeker finds he or she already has what is being sought but had not recognized it until the faeries pointed it out.

Even if you're not someone who journals about your spiritual progress, or no longer maintains a detailed Book of Shadows, I urge you to record the details of your journey and initiation into the ranks of the faery shamans. From this point forward the otherworlds will unfold to you in unique ways. Some will be obvious, others you will have to work hard to understand. In this initiation a plant spirit may say something you feel is too general or unremarkable to bother remembering. However, what seems at the time to be the most meaningless chatter can become of monumental importance days, weeks, or even years later.

Choosing Your Faery Shaman Name

If you were read fairy tales as a child you have some knowledge about the power in a name. "Rumplestiltskin" is a classic fairy tale you may recall from your childhood. It cautions you about the consequences of allowing someone else to know your true name, for in doing so you give away your power. If you know something or someone's true name, be it a name given at birth by humans or one bestowed by the deities, you gain a measure of control over that being's life. For this reason religious and indigenous people often take new names when they become spiritual adults.

Another reason, of course, was to remain anonymous if the religion you practiced was not in favor with the powers that be. No Jews openly used their Hebrew names in fifteenth-century Spain; no one openly used a Pagan name in sixteenth-century Europe, and no one openly used their Catholic confirmation names in England during the reign of the Protestant Reformation. When practicing the "wrong religion" was a crime, the fewer people who knew your true name, the better.

Most followers of the Craft choose a Craft name during our dedicant period of a year and a day, either keeping it or choosing another upon initiation. I was taught to have two additional Craft names. The first is a "surname" that does honor to your bloodlines and your faith, the second is one known only to you and the deities.

Choosing the correct name is an event to be taken seriously and with much consideration, for this is the name by which you will be known in the faery world from the time of your initiation onward. Most faeries are reluctant to reveal their true names. You will probably have to be content with using the name of the plant in which the plant spirit resides, or a false name the plant spirit wants you to call him or her. If a faery ever reveals its true name to you, take it as a high honor, a sign of perfect trust; never share that name with anyone else, not even other faeries.

Faery Alert

Pay attention if you feel a resonance with a certain plant and its spirit. Often, a nature spirit will appear or speak to you. Learn as much about the plant as you can, for this will teach you about the spirit that inhabits it.

Likewise, most humans use fake names when approaching the fey for the first time. This is similar to meeting an interesting stranger you think you might want to date, but giving out too much personal information right away is not the smart thing to do. If you disliked your given name as a child, here is your opportunity to not only change it, but to be known and addressed by a name of your choice by an entire realm of beings who accept this as your "real" name! In fact, it is your real name as far as the faeries—and any other astral world beings—are concerned. Think about the precedents for this change of names. It is a long-standing tradition to take a second name when your spiritual path goes in a new or an advanced direction. People take baptismal names, confirmation names, Jewish names, Wiccan names, and divination names. They also retain maiden names or change a last name to preserve the name of a specific clan whose name will die out in your own blood lines if someone does not legally adopt it and use it to carry on a cherished family name.

Many Pagans and New Agers take new names when they become involved in their new spiritual studies. Often these serious seekers take two names throughout their lifetimes. The first name may reflect an uninitiated or novice's feelings about the new path they are embarking on, and, as people grow and mature, a new name takes its place, one that the seeker has a deep sense of connection with and will keep for a lifetime. Those who change their spiritual names the way some people change deodorants often end up without a spiritual name because no one, neither fey nor human, can keep up with all the changes. Also, people tend to remember you by the first name by which you were introduced to them. I have friends whom I still call by names they discarded years ago, but, in my mind, that is who they are. When the time comes that these friends move so far beyond their old spiritual paths that I'm able to see them as different people, then I'm more easily able to make the transformation to call them by their birth names or new spiritual names.

When I was initiated into the religion of Wicca in 1981, I chose Shira as my new spiritual name. The name is Hebrew and means "a joyous song." Music has always played a large role in my life—in fact, I think my father gave his children not only names, but full background scores for our lives. I often hear a specific tune playing through the back of my mind in certain situations. I accept that this is the spirit of my father trying to reduce my current crisis with the soothing and empathetic song. I used Shira from 1981 until I changed it to a new spiritual name I have felt better suited to me in 1985.

Some seekers will take two spiritual names, one other spiritual seekers know them by, and another known only to the seeker, his or her deities, and perhaps the fey.

I prefer to have a different name to identify me as a faery shaman when I am in their world, or when they are conversing with me in my own world.

Such a name can reveal your deepest interests and commitment to the faery shaman's path. It can announce to faery, and to other beings on the astral plane, how you view yourself in your shamanic role. It also has its practical uses. If you are needed by a faery you have become close to, that faery can call you by that name and arouse you from the deepest sleep to come to your new friend's aid. If you are working with elemental beings— those of earth, water, fire, and air—or with nature spirits, they will not take advantage of knowing this name, but will use it to get your attention in the capacity of a faery shaman when your assistance is needed. Trust me, the first time that happens you will feel emotionally touched by this trust, and also scared that you might fail the faery who is depending on you for help. This is part of the process of spiritual growth. You will always encounter fears as you grow. These are tests to be passed so you can continue to grow and serve. Your faery friends will be there to help you. Go into your duties honestly and with as much confidence as you can muster. That is what will gain you the most respect from those you are trying to help.

Selecting Your Faery Shaman Name

We've already discussed the power inherent in a name, and when you choose a faery shaman name for yourself you will want to keep it something used by only you and the world of faery. Those who make their shaman names public often have a second name they use to identify themselves in the faery realm. You should choose a name that only the well-meaning faeries and those committed to the well-being of the inhabitants of many worlds will use to identify you. In turn, you will form bonds with faeries who will trust you with their "real" names. Until that time most faeries will identify themselves by the name of the plant, tree, or other foliage to which they are bound. Do not be insulted and do not beg to be trusted with a secret name before they are ready to tell you. They are only being cautious, and when we consider the way humankind has treated faeries and nature, they have every reason to be distrustful in the beginning. Be understanding of this natural hesitancy on their part. You will become good friends soon enough.

Because shamanism is a discipline all its own, one found in all cultures, it is not unusual for someone to take on a special shamanic name reserved for this specific type of spiritual work. This is especially the case in faery shamanism where names are an extension of the soul and can grant one power over any being whose true name is known to others.

As you begin to search for a faery shaman name by which you wish to be known in the world of faery, you may want to make notes of ideas that come into your head. You'll find them popping in at the most unwelcome moments, such as when you're driving your car or trying to stay awake during a meeting with your boss.

Whereas many spiritual seekers take all or part of the name of a deity or mythic hero, others take names from nature, or a combination of the two. One single name, simple and dignified, usually works best. Your fey friends are likely to go by only one name as well, and you don't want to appear pretentious.

You should discover your faery shaman name as soon as possible. When you enter into the guided meditation/astral projection where you will dedicate yourself to the faery shaman path, you will want to make your name and intention known to all you meet. The name can be changed later on if you feel a compelling need to do so.

Ideas can be culled from nature itself. You may want to take a flower name if you feel an affinity for flowers, or an herbal name if you are skilled at magickal or medicinal herbalism. Any name with one of the four elements, earth, water, fire, and air, is always appropriate. These can be attached to something more personal to you. You can also choose the name of a specific plant you use for healing brews. Only change that name if the nature spirit objects or you feel your deep association with that herb is inhibiting your growth as a faery shaman.

The examples here are meant to stimulate your creativity so you can arrive at your perfect faery shaman name. Some may be too long to use with ease, and others not descriptive enough to please you. Whatever name you decide on should feel right to you and please the inhabitants of the faery world:

Air Dancer
Airmid
Ancient Walker
Apple Blossom
Apple Seed
Autumn Touch
Avalon
Bluebells
Cauldron
Compassion
Cowslip
Culler
Destiny Heals
Dreamweaver
Duty Born
Earthkeeper
Earthman
Earthwoman
Everpresent
Faerywise
Far Walker
Fey Healer
Firefall
Follows the River
Forget-me-not

Foxglove
Ginger Ivy
Grannus
Greenkeeper
Harvester
Hawthorn
Healsong
Healing Hands
Lilac
Lily
Mighty Oak
Mullein
Musical Sage
Nature Student
Primrose
Pussywillow
Root Doctor
Silver Rain
Sirona
Soothes with Touch
Tea Maker
Willow Bark
Winged Wonder
Woodswise

Faery Alert

The need to play is part of the general character of nature spirits. But they may have another motivation too: to divert you, so that only the most insistent new shaman will reach his or her goal. Treat the fey as you would any friends who intrude too long on your working time. Tell them you have work to do and you will come back later to play. Then keep your promise. Once you have your faery shaman title and are doing good healing work, you can enjoy a play day with the faeries.

Preparing for Your Initiation

If you are a little nervous, you ought to reconsider whether this is the time or place for you to make this commitment. Maybe you have decided not to go through with the initiation today, but you just want to read it to gain a deeper understanding; that shows you are not viewing a partnership with faery as a game.

If you decide to initiate it yourself unguided by the structure of this book, here are some important points to remember about the initiation process:

- Some light music can help drown out ambient noise and make it easier to focus. Gary Stadler's faery music albums are my favorites, particularly the *Faery Heart Magick* album. Sometimes I use *Valley of the Sun's Ascension to All That Is*. Any music with a dreamy or indiscernible rhythm and no lyrics is helpful.
- Incense can be used to enhance your concentration, but keep it light. Faeries like jasmine, lavender, vanilla, rose, lilac, magnolia, and sweet pea.
- Be respectful of all beings you meet, but take abuse from none. If a faery or a band of faeries tries to stop you for too long just to play, you will need to be firm about your intent and your need to continue on. Be polite and sensitive to the faeries' feelings.
- Try to be aware by means of conversations to gauge how long you've been in the faery world. Don't ask the fey. They have almost no conception of time as we know it, so they won't answer, or, worse still, will make up a time line they think will please you.
- No matter how many times you've been a welcome visitor in their world, always ask permission each time to enter faeryland. You would expect this of anyone who entered your home. Give faery the same courtesy.
- If a being you encounter in the faery realm makes you feel uncomfortable or afraid, just move on, or come out of your meditation. You can leave the meditation quickly by saying the words, "I am home" to yourself. Then become aware of being inside your physical body and open your eyes. Remember, however, that what you fear may be what you most need to face.

- Call to your personal guardians, totem animals, and spirit guides if anything makes you afraid. They can get you out of faeryland in a heartbeat if it is necessary.
- Give yourself plenty of chances to turn back. No one will find fault with you for knowing when and if the life of a faery shaman is the right path for you.
- Don't ask a faery's true name, ask what he or she wishes to be called. Use a pseudonym for yourself until mutual trust is built.
- Do not be startled to see faeries other than plant spirits. Interact with them if you want, but stay focused on your goal.
- Few faeries, if any, will be able to come back with you to the physical world. Some, however, may show up at your hearth or in your garden later on. Remember to offer them food and drink.
- Repeat your goal of becoming a faery shaman to everyone you meet.
- Be prepared to answer tough questions about your goal and why you wish to be a faery shaman.
- Faeries will tempt you to stay with food, drink, and material treasures. Do not become enamored of these gifts. It is not usually advisable to eat, drink, or dance with the faeries. These are their greatest pleasures, but it is too easy to lose track of how long you've been away in faeryland or even what your original purpose for being there was.

Faery Tales

Many faery shamans come from Celtic, Anglo-Saxon, or Nordic backgrounds, where it was customary to offer guests food and drink. Denying hospitality even to one's enemy was an unforgivable oversight. Mythology tells us that warring parties would sleep under the same roof and eat at the same table bound by the rules of hospitality. We are also told the ugly consequences for those who did not respect this custom. Because of these traditions, some faery shamans have retreated from the cautionary advice about taking food or drink from the fey because they fear being seen as rude or possibly harmful. Use your own judgment.

The Guided Meditation for the Initiation
of the Faery Shaman

The format for your initiation as a faery shaman will be a detailed guided meditation. Whether you view this sort of pathworking as going outside of yourself or deep within, know that these places and their inhabitants are real. The connections you forge, the manner in which you are treated, and the aftershocks you experience in your world of normal consciousness will let you know you are dealing with real forces, elemental powers that cannot be controlled by you. This is why partnership, friendship, and common goals are essential. The faery shaman is the most important faery partner of them all.

We will do this initiation using an astral projection metaphor. Whether you are talented at astral projection or think you can't do it, you will experience the full impact of the faery shaman initiation. The only people who do not complete this journey are those who decide to turn back. Some are told by the guardians of the gateway to faeryland or by one of the elemental rulers that they are not yet ready to take on the faery shaman task. They may decide to wait until later, or never opt to commit to the path of the faery shaman.

If possible, have someone read the meditation aloud to you with a group of other magickal-minded people. This means not only Pagans, but New Agers, Kabbalists, Gnostics, spiritual seekers, and shamans from all cultures. The collective consciousness in such a group is huge and palpable. Being in this company is a boon to healing efforts because magickally-minded people have a keen awareness of the energies surrounding them, especially in groups. The healing energy spreads from person to person when we are with people who share our interests in and perceptions of the universe. When we feel safe and let our outer guards down, the best healing takes place.

If that's not possible, you may record this meditation and play it back as needed. You might want to record it over soothing music to help slow your mind and make you more receptive. If you prefer, read it to yourself or memorize its high points and take off on your own. Experiment and do whatever works best for you.

Only the plain text is read out loud. The words in parentheses are instructions or notations for when and how long to pause for action and verbal exchanges in the meditation so you don't feel rushed. The same is true for the headings of Step 1, Step 2, etc. In this type of meditation you are entering another world and the process should never be broken into parts, but used as a whole, both to allow you to go deeply into other-worlds and so you will not be as likely to be jolted out of those worlds by the noises in your physical world which can distract you. It is one whole process. The breakdowns are used here for easy reference if you want to go back to examine the details of any specific section another time.

You should do all in your power to stay focused on your goal and not allow outside sounds or thoughts to distract you. Ear plugs that block out high decibel sounds can be priceless to a modern spiritual seeker, and they can be found in any drugstore and will not blow your budget. In the beginning maybe only one part of your astral self is entering the otherworld, but soon you will be a skilled shaman, a traveler between worlds. Focus on your successes, not on your setbacks.

Now we begin the journey. Make sure this is what you really want to do before you begin. Go. Believe. Enjoy and work. Teach and learn.

Step 1

Close your eyes and relax your body. You may sit or recline, but choose a position you can remain in comfortably for up to an hour. Crossing your legs or arms can cause numbness that will draw your attention from the world of faery. You may want something to support your lower back, shoulders, or neck. We each have our areas of weakness, so take your time when choosing your preferred position for guided meditation, or any other kind.

Step 2

Breathe slowly and center yourself. As you begin to fully relax your body, focus your mind on your goal of entering the world of faery. There you will obtain from a faery a talisman you will wear whenever you enter their world; it will identify you as a faery shaman. Most faeries welcome their shaman, even if grudgingly.

Step 3

You are now going to astrally project into the realm of faery because faery is the closest world to ours on the astral plane. This realm overlaps and interpenetrates our own, but we have been trained for centuries not to see it. It is also a state of mind, one you slip into whenever you are mentally absorbed in some activity. This is the way your consciousness leaves your physical body for a time and ventures forth to have experiences on its own.

As a shaman, you will be a faery seer in all senses of that word. You will leave and return through the crown chakra, or energy center, at the top of the head. If you have a method you already use for entering the land of faery, you may go ahead now and wait for the rest of us at its gates. If you are taking this trip alone, please skip to the place where the guardians of the gates of faery challenge you with questions before you are either allowed to enter or turned away.

Step 4
Continue breathing slowly and deeply, in through your nose and out through your mouth. Feel the numbing sensation beginning in your feet as your astral body pulls itself upward from your feet. They may tingle for a moment, then you should become unaware of them. They are not needed where you are going. The spiritual essence of yourself is preparing to leave its earthly body. It is not needed on this journey, and it will remain where it is and safe until you choose to return.

Step 5
Continue bringing your astral self up through your calves, knees, and thighs. As your astral self passes through these areas, become unaware that they were ever a part of you. Keep pulling your astral self up to the root chakra at the base of your tailbone. Feel your astral self pass this center that connects you to the earth world and become unaware of it. Pull your astral body from the root chakra up to your navel center just below your belly button. Allow it to pass through as it continues to travel upward through your earth body. At this point you should be fully relaxed and disconnected from any awareness of or sensation in any place below your waist.

Step 6
Your astral self now knows where it is going in order to escape your body, and it travels quickly up through your solar plexus into the heart center in the middle of your chest. Allow your fingers, hands, and arms

to go numb as you pull your astral self out of them, and let your complete astral body be at your throat chakra.

From the neck down you should feel you have no physical self. Dismiss all thoughts of the physical as your astral self rapidly rises to the psychic center called your third eye chakra, immediately above and between your eyes. Take a moment to make sure your astral self is fully collected there, then push it to the center of the top of your head, and outside your body.

If you feel the need, take one last look at your physical self to assure you that it is alive and protected while you are gone.

Step 7

Thought is action in the astral realm, and the world of faery lies somewhere between the earth world and the astral world. Visualize yourself being at the edge of a dense, green forest. This forest is the first area you must cross in order to reach the realm of the elemental rulers of the faery world. Take just a moment to think once again about your goal of becoming a faery shaman. If you are uncertain, you may turn back now.

Step 8

Step into the forest and feel yourself immediately enveloped in the cool green world of the old forest. Listen to the sounds of the air in the trees, the chirping of the birds, the scurrying of small animals on the ground and in the trees around you. You feel very safe and protected in this forest, just as if you were inside the womb of Mother Earth.

Step 9

Proceed through the forest, taking note of any faery beings or animals which appear to you, as these may become important totems or allies for you later.

Step 10

Up ahead you see light, and you realize the forest is ending. As you reach its edge you find an enchanting creek running past with lots of stepping stones for you to use to get to the other side. Walk slowly and carefully. You do not want to disturb any water faeries or animals. Take note of lily pads and other water foliage that might try to attract your attention.

Step 11

As you walk up the small bank on the other side of the creek, you see before you a large meadow-like prairie, full of tall grass and wild flowers waving in the wind. These are not high enough to keep you from seeing some sort of gateway in the far distance, so you start out through the meadow with the gateway as your goal. Take note of any animals or plant faeries present or who try to get your attention. These may be very important contacts later on.

Step 12

As you get closer to the gateway you can tell it is an entrance to faeryland, one reserved for high-ranking seekers. Two large flames guard the entrance. Next to them are two massive dragon-dogs. As you approach the gateway they cross two sharp spears across the entrance, making an X. Keep in mind the saying, "X marks the spot," and remain confident about your goal.

Step 13

The dragon-dogs have three questions for you:

"By what name are you known?" they ask in low, loud, and vibrant voices.

(Pause to allow the faery shaman seeker to decide and reply to the question using whatever name feels correct to him or her.)

"Whom do you serve?" they ask.

(Pause while the seeker answers. The customary answers are connected to spiritual traditions; however, you can be spiritual without being religious. Some traditional answers are "I serve God," or "I serve the Goddess." Other appropriate answers are "I serve Mother Earth" or "I serve all beings in life or death" or "I serve where my help is most needed." Whatever your answer, it will be a fact faery will file on you permanently, so choose wisely.)

"What do you seek here?" the dragon-dogs ask.

(Pause while the seeker makes his or her first statement about his or her desire to become a faery shaman.)

Step 14

At this point you may be turned away if the guardians of faery think you are not able to do the job, or if they feel you are not ready to take on this responsibility at this time. The seeker may wish to add some qualifying information if the guardians are hesitant to permit entry. If they still deny entry, then go home by the same route through which you entered and, if you choose, try this mediation again later.

Those who are permitted entrance are told, "You may enter for the good of all and harm to none, merry meet."

Step 15

As the spears are withdrawn and you walk through the entryway of the faery shaman you may say thank you, or any other acknowledgment you wish to give to the guardians.

Inside the flaming gateway you are greeted by some elven faeries who offer you food and drink. You may partake or not as you choose.

If you turn them down, explain that you are not being rude, you are just focused on your mission of becoming a faery shaman, and you will be delighted to share a celebratory drink with them as soon as you have done what you came to do. Faery feelings are easily bruised, and their retribution is much worse than the offense warrants, so, if the fey seem miffed even after your explanation, promise them a time and place you will meet with them. Keep in mind that once you are accepted as a faery shaman, your rapport with faery will be different, and more faeries will appear to you who wish to be serious than who wish to play games, tricks, or to entrap you. This promise should satisfy them, just be sure to follow through. Be where you said you would be, when you said you would be there. Time may have no meaning in faery, but they will know you kept your promise even if they botched the details on their end.

(Pause for the seeker to eat, drink, and speak with the faeries.)

The faeries who brought you the food and drink disappear quickly, perhaps offering you a word of luck on your journey.

Step 16

Now that you are inside the realm of faery, you notice ahead of you a steep, grassy hillside. A well-worn path staggers up the hill, the top of which is obscured from your vantage point. Knowing this is the route you must take, you begin to ascend the hill. With each step you take, impress firmly on your mind your desire to leave this realm as a newly initiated faery shaman.

Step 17

As you travel up the hill you hear not only the noises expected in nature, but also faery voices. The Dryads, the strong spirits of the trees, are always asking seekers to stop and play. If you feel like pausing to play, you may do so, but if you tell them your goal they will respect it and will not try to detain you further. After all, their survival and yours are linked.

As you continue to climb you hear some faeries cheering you on, other individuals who tell you they don't want your help, and others who sing to you. Faery song weaves a strong enchantment. It can enslave, empower, or liberate. Do not become so attached to its beauty that you have trouble leaving this hill. You can always come back later.

Step 18

The landscape changes as you near the top of the hill. At the summit you see the lavish and opulent thrones of the four elemental rulers. Behind each of them the scenery appropriate to their season can be seen.

The Gnome King sits to the north. In the hierarchy of faery, the Gnome King most often comes out as the supreme ruler. Gnomes are of the earth element. Down the hill behind him, as far as you can see, is a winter landscape in which all life has been carefully protected or tucked away for winter. The Gnomes you see working in this world are chopping wood and foraging for food for animals who do not hibernate in winter. A large frozen lake sparkles in the sunshine, one that promises a wealth of knowledge and entertainment.

To your right is the throne of the Queen of the Sylphs, the elementals of the air. Down the hill behind her, as far as you can see, it is springtime. Blossoming trees, newborn flowers, lovers gazing into one another's eyes, all promise an interesting adventure.

Step into the circle of thrones so you can see the King of the Salamanders, the elementals of fire. Behind him is a summer landscape. The sun is bright and intense, all of nature is in its full glory, and the woodlands and farms promise an interesting excursion.

To the west sits the beautiful Undine Queen, the ruler of the element of water and all the fey who are of this element. Behind her, down the hill, you see a landscape of autumn beauty, crisp fall weather, and bright blue skies. A walk through the piles of fallen leaves, some in which you see faeries at play, seems very enticing.

Step 19

Beginning with the Gnome King, introduce yourself and state your intention of becoming initiated as a faery shaman. Like all the elemental rulers, he may ask you questions about your experience and intent. Answer him honestly, for in the realm of faery a lie is one of the greatest disgraces, one sure to get you booted out of their world. This is why faeries often speak in riddles. They cannot lie, but they are very good at walking all around the truth without ever stepping on it.

The Gnome King appears as stoic and stable as the earth element he represents, and you feel comfortable in his presence. Under his intense brown-eyed gaze you feel secure, empowered, yet humbled. His world promises you great enlightenment, and the opportunity to make a major impact on all nature with your good intentions. Ask his permission to enter his world and seek your talisman of shamanic healing power. He may answer you now, or he may tell you to wait until you have been introduced to all the elemental rulers before he makes his decision.

(Pause to allow time for the seeker to speak with the Gnome King before continuing with the meditation.)

Step 20

Turn to your right and present yourself to the Queen of the Sylphs. Her smile may seem capricious, as this is the nature of the element. Her landscape is windy and wild, promising unexpected diversions. You know her world will have many obstacles to your goal, but it is worth exploring. State your intention of leaving this world as a faery shaman and obtaining a talisman marking you as one. Ask permission to enter her world. She may answer now, or she may wait until you have been presented to all the elemental rulers.

(Pause to allow time for the seeker's audience with the Queen of the Sylphs before continuing with the meditation.)

Step 21

The next ruler you face is the Salamander King on his fiery throne of gold. When you look into his topaz eyes you can see every desire of your heart reflected there. Behind him is what you might call the Summerland, the eternal home of young and beautiful spirits. The heat of a summer day assails you as you speak with him, and memories of pleasant summers of childhood rush through your mind. State your intention of coming here to obtain a talisman marking you as a faery shaman. Ask his permission to come into his world. He may answer you now, or he may wait until you have spoken with the Undine Queen.

(Pause so the seeker may speak with the Salamander King before continuing with the meditation.)

Step 22

The Undine Queen is cordial, if moody, and seems to be able to see the most profound feelings you've ever experienced. Behind her the world is in a constantly changing state of autumn. You know this is where the powers of the empath are given, a dubious honor. You also see faeries playing in crystal clear pools of water, and others dancing on the surf of a green ocean shoreline. Make your statement to her about your desire to become a faery shaman and to obtain a talisman. Ask permission to enter her world. She may answer you now, or she may defer the decision to the Gnome King.

(Pause for the seeker to speak with the Undine Queen before continuing the meditation.)

Step 23

At this point the Kings and Queens will tell you if you are welcome in the realm of faery. It is unusual for one element to deny you access if the others admit you, but if this happens respect that ruler's reasoning and revisit the issue another time.

Once you have been given permission to enter the realm of faery, or of one or more of their elements, you may choose one path to explore in your quest. Before you begin, the Gnome King rises and places his right hand on your left shoulder. You realize you are expected to do the same to him. You stand face to face in the position of crossed pathways, star-crossed events, and the bonds of your promises. The Gnome King asks you one more time what it is you seek. Let him know that you have thought long and hard about it, and you desire to become a faery shaman.

(You may change your mind if you like, and some kindly faery will escort you back to the entrance of dragon-dogs and flames. You may always come back and make your attempt another time.)

The Gnome King acknowledges your goal.

(He may turn you back, telling you either: 1–You are not ready to become a faery shaman at this time, or, 2–The path of the faery shaman is not the one for you in this lifetime, but to rethink what you seek and ask help from your spirit guides and deities to find your proper path in this life. You may have to make the statement of your goal as many as nine times before receiving any answer. Repeat your goal as many times as feels right to you and which honors the path you are currently following in this lifetime. If the answer is still no, thank all the rulers, then turn back toward home and your waiting body. You can always try again later, even if you've been told the role of faery shaman is not your life's path. Many things change the direction of our lives, and what is true today may be false tomorrow.)

The Gnome King nods, and you see a faint smile raise wrinkles on his genial face. He is proud to welcome another initiate to faery. Your willingness to take on this job means one more ally the fey have in their mission to keep Mother Earth and all her children alive.

(Pause so the seeker can look around the circle of thrones one last time and thank the rulers for their time, even those who may not have permitted entrance to their element. They have their reasons. Perhaps their element is one you are already strong in, and you need the challenge of seeking your faery shaman talisman elsewhere. Or they may feel you are not well-grounded in their element, and that you will find your talisman with greater ease in another element. Also, any ruler may feel you and he or she just are not resonating together at this time. As you grow as a faery shaman the elements now closed to you will open. In the meantime you can do exercises and meditations to help you connect with this missing element.)

Step 24

Look around you at all four of the enticing landscapes. If a spirit guide or totem animal appears to you, you may ask it for assistance in choosing a direction. You want to go to the place where you will be given the proper talisman.

(Pause for a moment or two to allow the seeker to make a decision.)

As you make your choice you feel a burst of confidence in your step, and you start happily down the hill into the landscape you have chosen to explore, the one you feel holds the talisman that will for now and ever identify you to the faeries and to others on the path of the faery shaman, as someone who walks between the worlds with them.

Step 25

As you head down the hill into your chosen landscape you notice the land levels out faster than expected. As you stop and look around you find a multitude of interesting things from the natural world vying for your attention. You may hear your name being called, or hear blessings on your path being offered to you. Acknowledge each as you feel is appropriate.

You are on a mission to find the talisman, to be obtained from a faery or group of faeries, that will identify you as a faery shaman. Announce your desire to all beings you meet or who speak to you from hidden recesses in the landscape. The fey will know you are there by permission of their rulers, and that your job is vital to your mutual survival.

(Pause for a moment for this exchange of communication.)

Step 26

A faery being may appear to you and offer to take you to the place where your talisman is waiting. You may ask him or her questions. Listen to the answers with your head as well as your heart. Faeries cannot lie to you, but they can circumvent the truth with great skill.

(Pause for several minutes to allow the seeker to question the faeries and make decisions based on their answers.)

Go with these faeries if you wish. Telling them you have another direction in mind if you don't like their responses to your questions will cause you no harm. These faeries know your quest is important, but they may feel like playing right now, thinking you can come back another day for your talisman.

Whether you are being taken in hand by faeries, or going on instinct alone, focus your thoughts on your goal of becoming a faery shaman. Repeat it out loud or in your head like a mantra in order to keep you going forward on the correct path. Take all the time you need. You may even feel led to go into the landscape of another element, or to the border of two elements to find your talisman. If anyone is with you, feel free to ask questions about your search. You may get gibberish, or you may cut your search time. You might even be taken through a landscape to which you will be asked, or you will want, to return to later.

(Pause for two or three minutes for the seeker to find his or her way to the faery plant spirit who will offer the talisman.)

Step 27

Use your shamanic intuition and go where it leads you. By now many nature spirits will be making themselves known to you. You will know the right one to go to when you see him or her, or when he or she calls to you.

(Pause to allow time for the seeker to telepathically communicate with the faeries.)

As you approach the tree, leaf, flower, herb, weed, grass, or other place from which the faery is calling you, state again your goal of becoming a faery shaman and ask if he or she is the nature spirit for whom you are looking.

(This faery may only have a personal message for the seeker, or it may be his/her job to point the seeker in the right direction. The faery may also ask again if the seeker wishes to continue or go back. Pause for a minute or two to allow this exchange to take place.)

After this conversation, you should follow the faery's instructions.

(Pause to allow seeker to sit, go elsewhere, turn back, or whatever he or she chooses to do.)

Step 28

When you feel you are in the presence of the nature spirit who will bestow on you the talisman of the faery shaman, you may ask if this is the case. The answer is usually yes. If not, take a moment to go where you have been instructed to go. Only disobey the request if you feel a sense of danger or you believe the nature spirit is sending you away from your goal, not toward it.

The right nature spirit will come to stand in front of you. No matter how tall or short he or she is, he or she will manage to be eye to eye with you. Once again you are asked your goal. Answer as you feel is correct. If you remain you will be given the talisman of the faery shaman, and there is no turning back. Be patient if the nature spirit asks you about your decision more than once. You are taking on a huge responsibility, and the fey do not deal well with slackers.

(This is your last chance to turn back. Thank the nature spirit for its words and leave if you must. There is no shame in knowing what you can and cannot commit to doing.)

Step 29

You remain eye to eye with the nature spirit, almost as if you are assessing one another's souls. Your posture, eye contact, and determination will show more than words can tell that you are ready to take on this task.

The faery asks you, "By what name do you wish to be called?"

Give the nature spirit the name you gave the dragon-dogs when you entered faeryland, or use another if something along your journey has sparked an idea for a new name for you. Tell the faery what you wish to be called.

(Pause for the seeker to say the name and for the faery to repeat it back.)

The nature spirit speaks to you again, and as he or she does, more fey may gather near you or peek out from behind their foliage. Beginning with the faery shaman name you have chosen earlier in this chapter, the spirit will speak to you.

(Pause to allow the faery to give a clue to the seeker if he or she has fey blood. If the seeker wants to go on this trek in search of fey family now, discourage it. Continue on with the meditation. This is the time for committing to others. Finding one's own spiritual roots should be left for another time.)

"_____, (the faery will state the name you have chosen to use as your faery shaman name), you have come of your own free will to the realm of faery, the home of the healing nature spirits. We live here between the world of faery and the world of humanity, belonging not wholly to one or another. We are as close to your world as any being of another realm can be, but closer to the divine creator than your world. You have honored us by coming here with a clear head, a strong heart, and the determination to become a faery shaman. If this is truly your goal, and you seek it only for the highest good, then say so you now."

(Pause for only a moment to answer the nature spirit.)

"From this time forward you will be our partner, our equal, known to the healing spirits of our world as _____(faery shaman name). Our first task is to save our Mother Earth from extinction. The second goal is to heal others from any realm who seek our help. We heal the spirit and we heal the emotions, and lastly do we seek to heal our own physical bodies. Unselfish service to others is the highest goal either of us can achieve. Will you take from me this talisman to seal and symbolize the agreement forged between us this day?"

Step 30

The nature spirit will offer you a talisman of some kind, one the faeries of this place have agreed upon to represent your commitment to work with them. Take it and say your thanks, then repeat again your pledge of partnership.

At this point you should internalize the talisman in some way. If it is something you feel you should carry through the worlds in between, like a wand or staff, you should visualize it melding into your arms. If it is a stone, leaf, or other small object, pull it into your heart center or solar plexus area. It will be visible only in the otherworlds. If you are given jewelry, wear it as requested, and feel it melding with your astral body. It, too, will be visible only in the faery realms. You can decide if, when, and how to make an earth plane version of what you are given.

Step 31

When you feel you have gleaned all you can from this encounter, say your farewells, and start back toward the hill where the thrones of the four elemental rulers sit in wait for you.

As you arrive they stand to greet you, acknowledging that you are equals in a partnership with the same goals. Allow them each to speak with you, and for each to bestow upon you his or her specific initiation as a faery shaman.

(Pause for at least five minutes to allow time for this. This is one of the most emotional and moving experiences the new shaman will ever encounter.)

Step 32

When you have been fully initiated as a faery shaman, say your thank yous and goodbyes once more, then head back down the hill toward the fire-flanked gateway. As you approach the dragon-dog guardians cross their spears over the gateway once again.

They ask, "Who is it who seeks to pass through these gates?"

You reply, "I am a faery shaman fulfilling my obligations."

The guardians see your talisman, nod to acknowledge their respect, and remove their spears. From now on the only thing you will need to reenter or to exit this realm is your talisman.

Step 33

You travel back across the prairie with the wind at your back, feeling elated and charged with a new sense of purpose. When you come to the creek, you see that a small bridge has been placed there for you to use, which disappears from view as you walk up the bank on the other side. As your joyful steps bounce you through the forest, a host of nature spirit life calls out to you, some acknowledging your newly forged partnership, others introducing themselves for the first time. Nod to acknowledge them all and promise to return soon.

Step 34

When you reach the end of the forest, stop. Turn to look back at the woodland once more so you will always remember exactly where to come when you wish to return. Mentally close your eyes and feel your astral body lift away from this world in between and return to the crown chakra at the top of your head.

Step 35

Take a deep breath, and begin to allow your astral body to sink back into the confines of your physical self. As it does, visualize your crown chakra turning a clear violet, clean and pure. Bring the astral into your third eye chakra and visualize it glowing a rich indigo.

As you bring your astral self into your throat chakra it throbs with a deep blue.

You are becoming aware once more that you have a physical body. Allow your astral self to settle back into your arms, hands, and fingers. Flex your fingers as your consciousness returns to them.

Take your astral body down through your vibrant green heart chakra, and into the yellow brightness of your solar plexus. You begin to be aware again of the room your physical body has been waiting in, and your astral body—knowing where it belongs—sinks into your sparkling orange navel chakra, and on into the vibrating red chakra at the base of your tailbone.

Step 36

As your astral self reconnects with your legs, feet, and toes, allow your higher self to adjust your freshly cleansed chakras to the size they should be, somewhere between fully opened and fully closed. Take another deep cleansing breath. Stretch your limbs and open your eyes. You are home, back in your earth plane home, but very aware that you now carry the responsibility, the talisman, and the title of faery shaman.

Returning from the Faery Realm

In order to feel fully back in your normal waking consciousness, to feel a sense of peace and closure, and so that unwanted astral entities cannot follow you back home, there are traditional methods of awakening from a shamanic journey that have been used for thousands of years. One of the easiest things to do is eat. Even if you've "eaten" in the astral world, your physical body has not been fed. The urge to eat and the process of eating is one of the most primitive instincts we possess, one that only living beings do.

Some people like to shower or bathe, a way of washing away any debris which may have followed you from the otherworld, and also a way to "ground" excess psycho-spiritual energy away from you. This residue is not something you want to carry around. It can make you nervous, attract lower astral entities, and just gives you and everyone around you the jitters.

The popularity of meditation and journeying has taken the concept of grounding from an abstract to an actual practice. Many people need to discharge energy residue onto the earth. Place your palms flat against the ground, a stone, or a tree. Remain there until you feel relaxed and ready to resume your daily living.

6

Elemental Work and Faeries

Becoming a faery shaman entails more than just knowing faery as housemates or gaming partners. You do not have to be an expert at any New Age art to have a successful initiation as a faery shaman. However, a spiritual connection with nature and the elements is helpful. In this chapter you will learn about the elements and how to work with them.

Uniting with the Elements

As you make friends with the faeries you will also find yourself attracted to plants, trees, or places that resonate with one particular element. In the Western Pagan mystery traditions the elements are usually earth, air, fire, and water. Sometimes the element of spirit is added to that list, as the element that unites the other four.

Pay attention to your own responses to water, earth, fire, or the wind. How do you feel when you sit beside a stream or walk through a forest or warm yourself at a fireplace? Does being in the presence of one particular element cause a special leap in your soul? This element connects you to the faery kingdom and it is the best place for you to begin forging your bond with faery. If you have had a lifelong fear of fire or water, start your learning with the elements of air and earth, while you try to find out the root cause of your phobia. The elemental rulers you will meet on your guided meditation can be of enormous help if you just ask them.

During the Middle Ages, when alchemy and other protosciences were beginning to merge with magickal thought, the sixteenth-century occultist, Cornelius Agrippa, wrote the following about the nature of the four elements in the first of his three books on occult philosophy:

> "There are four elements . . . of which all elemented inferior bodies are compounded; not by way of heaping them together, but by transmutation [change into another substance still made up of elemental components] and union; and when they are destroyed, they are resolved into elements. For there is none of the sensible elements that is pure, but they are more or less mixed, and apt to be changed one into the other . . . And this is the root and foundation of all bodies, natures, virtues, and wonderful works; and he which shall know these qualities of the elements, and their mixations, shall easily bring to pass such things that are new and we shall be perfect in magick."

In the exercises that follow we are going to find places where elements overlap. For example, is a volcano earth or fire? We will allow the rulers of the elements to help us. Please use your common sense if you go into nature and try these experiments. Some things are not safe to do alone, and there are many places where it is not safe to let down your awareness of your surroundings.

Taking Note of Your Position with the Sentient Elements

We all have elements in which we feel most at home. We also have some with which we feel less comfortable. This may be connected to our birth charts, our early environments, our past-life memories, our current environments, or just an affinity with an as yet undetermined source.

On a piece of paper make four columns for the elements and head them earth, air, fire, and water. Under each heading write the name of something in your world that strikes you as being closely related to that element. Other people, even characteristics of your own personality, might remind you of a particular element. Note all the correspondences that come to mind. Take your time compiling this list. It will tell you more about yourself than you think. When you have finished your list, read it over, make any changes, and look for overlaps between elements.

Next, contemplate the various aspects of your life: home, family, friends, work, school, commuting, exercising, sports, hobbies, bad habits, strengths, weaknesses, etc. As you analyze your completed list, see if any one area of your life seems weighted more toward one element than the others. This is not a bad thing. Most of us have a special affinity for one or two of the elements.

Faery Tales

"The existence of Faery Healers and Faery Doctors in the Celtic tradition provides a direct link back to a much earlier era of human history. . . . Human history is full of [faery] magick all cultures have used it."
—Margie McArthur, *Faery Healing: The Lore and the Legacy*

Count the number of entries in each column and compare them. Just how weighted toward one element is your list? Can you think of other things in your life that you are leaving out of the list that might fall under the other elements? It is not unusual to overlook things in your life that you do not enjoy as much.

If there is a marked difference, allow the elemental rulers to help you find a better balance. For example, if you like to cook, camp, and set off fireworks you are an obvious fire person. Adding one of the other elements to balance you takes simple logic. Adding air will fan your fire out of control. Water your fire and you have steam. Put earth on your fire, or your fire on your earth, and you produce a warm environment that feels safe. Fire warms your earth, earth puts out your fire.

Another way to assess your elemental personality is by casting your horoscope. All of the twelve signs of the zodiac have an element to which they belong.

- **Air Signs:** Gemini, Libra, Aquarius
- **Fire Signs:** Aries, Leo, Sagittarius
- **Water Signs:** Cancer, Scorpio, Pisces
- **Earth Signs:** Taurus, Virgo, Capricorn

Your personal birth chart will also show where other planets in our solar system were at the moment of your birth. If enough of these are of one specific element, or if you were born between two signs, another element may rule your behavior and the type of healing faeries who are attracted to you.

Bringing your life into balance will make you a happier, healthier person, and a better healer. Keep in mind that there is no quick fix, however. One treatment is not enough. Enjoy your time with the elements you add to your life and see if you don't notice a change for the better in both health and happiness.

Balancing the Elemental You

If you cannot, or would rather not, find a place in nature to commune with the elements, you can do so via astral projection. Each approach has its own lessons to teach. The first time I reveled in the elements was on an assignment from my Craft teacher twenty years ago. I mixed the earth plane and astral planes then, and still do. The goal is not to master or take control of the element, though some advanced magick practices do this. Instead we are choosing to understand the unique qualities of each element and the nature spirits who call it home.

In this exercise you will return to faeryland through the gates of fire as you did for your faery shaman initiation. You will climb the hill again and ask to speak to one of the elemental rulers about developing a deeper link to the element they represent. I know of no one who has been turned away. The elementals know how crucial our help and concern are to their survival. They are thrilled by each new faery shaman who comes to them and asks to better connect with and understand the power of the elements.

You may start with whomever you wish to ask first. For simple continuity I will discuss them in the same order as in the guided meditation, beginning with north and earth, then moving clockwise around the circle of thrones.

Understanding the Element of Earth
Your first stop is at the throne of the Gnome King in the north. Tell him what you want to do, then pause to see how he chooses to help you. He

may send you along into his astral faery world for a while, or direct you to learn about his element on the earth plane. He may ask you to watch—really watch—as forest land and farm fields are destroyed to make room for gas stations, strip malls, or housing developments. He may ask you to return to him as soon as you have completed your earth-learning exercises, or he may appear to you on the earth plane when you are finished in his realm. Keep your "twilight eyes" open so you can see him.

Some of the things the Gnome King may ask you to do might seem odd, but when you speak with him later about your education, he will be pleased that you kept an open mind. If there is no safe place where you live to carry out his instructions, then go by astral body into faery-land to learn; there you will be safe.

Here are some things you can do to understand the earth element better and learn to work with it productively:

- Plant a garden, one of your own, or communally with other like-minded people.
- Help out on a charitable housing construction project in your community, such as Habitat for Humanity.
- Visit a greenhouse or garden center and familiarize yourself with different types of soil. How do they feel and smell?
- Learn about different herbs and plants, their medicinal uses, their folk magick values. Notice your responses to them—which ones do you feel drawn to?
- Learn about burrowing animals and the animals who walk on the forest floor. Try to understand what encroachment on their land and the erosion of their food sources is doing to the balance of our ecosystem.
- Find ways to recycle household products that would otherwise end up in a landfill.
- Become outraged at the way Mother Earth is being treated. Stand up and fight for her as you would for your human mother.
- Pick up litter and clean up graffiti.
- Lie in a bed of freshly plowed earth. Feel how cool and damp it is beneath you. Let the nature spirits of earth come to chat with you. Ask them any questions you like and answer theirs.

- Avoid using toxic chemicals to keep down weeds or make your lawn greener. These endanger animals, including pets, and it ends up in our drinking water. Consult an authority on organic gardening to learn about safe alternatives.
- Play among the trees in a dense forest.
- Start a game of hide and seek with the earth elementals in the woods.
- Try to visit places where the element of earth manifests abundantly.
- Sit quietly in your own home and try to connect with the earth elementals in your own environment.
- Alone, with earth nature spirits, or with the Gnome King, consider ways you can use the earth element for healing. Burying an illness or grounding energy are two possibilities.

Wear essential oils of earthy scents, such as patchouli, cedar, and pine, to keep you in touch with the earth element. As you inhale the soft scent, evoke the power of the element with the words:

> Blesséd earth beneath my feet,
> At the juncture of two worlds we meet;
> Ready am I to do your healing,
> Fill me now with your powerful feeling.
> Earth of magick and of the fey,
> Earth stay with us night and day;
> Solid earth in which healing is held fast,
> Help me to take only the need I ask.

Understanding the Element of Air

Present yourself to the Sylph Queen and ask her how you can best learn to understand her element and its power. She may direct you to specific places in her world. After you have completed immersing yourself in her element, she may wish to speak with you again.

Here are some ways you can familiarize yourself with the air element, so you can work with it effectively:

- Become aware of the air quality where you live. Chart it over the course of a year to see when and why it fluctuates.

- Stand facing a strong breeze and feel the wind rush past you. Then turn around and feel the wind at your back.
- Be conscious of the air quality in any place where you spend a lot of time. If you can't open the windows in your workplace, take breaks outdoors so you can breathe different air.
- Heed your community's pollution warnings and cooperate with efforts to keep pollution to a minimum, especially during summer.
- Watch how the wind causes tall trees to dance and twist.
- Take note of how the wind directs the rain during a downpour.
- Raise your arms to the wind and imagine you can fly!
- Think of places where the element of air is manifested powerfully in your world.
- Fly a kite. Draw a sylph, or faery air elemental, on it to let the fey of the air know you are learning all you can about their world.
- Fly an ultralight plane or glider if you have the money and the nerve.
- Take a ride in a hot air balloon.
- Watch birds.
- Gaze up at clouds.
- Either alone, with the nature spirits of air, or with the Sylph Queen for company, come up with as many ways to heal with air as you can. Blowing away negative energies attached to you is one possibility.

Burn incense that helps you connect with the element of air. Florals such as lilac, rose, jasmine, and lavender are good choices. Use this, or a similar evocation to the element as you inhale the soft scent:

Spirits of healing in well-blown air,
Come into my garden fair;
I call on you to help me find,
The healing path for one of my kind.
Spirits of air, borne on the wind,
Capricious and wild, as trees to it bend;
Lend me your power to heal and calm,
And to do what I must without any harm.

Understanding the Element of Fire

Next, present yourself to the King of the Salamanders. Ask him to help you understand how his element works in your world and in your own environment. Like the other rulers, he may direct you to a place within his faery world, or give you suggestions for work you can do in or near your own home. If you have a balefire (sacred bonfire) pit or a fireplace you can do much fire work in the comfort of your own home. (Remember never to leave any fire unattended.)

Here are some ways you can learn about the element of fire and how to best use its energy.

- Sit and watch a fire burn. This can be a bonfire, a fireplace, or a simple candle. Notice how the flame moves. (Making it bend with just your will is a great magickal exercise!)
- Hold your palms as close as you comfortably can to the flame and feel what the fire is teaching you.
- Focus on the transformative powers of fire. These changes usually happen very fast. When something needs a radical change fire can metaphorically burn down the old so the new can flourish.
- Use your hands to make a flame dance. Do not burn yourself, tip the candle over, or forget the purpose of this exercise.
- Think of places on earth where the element of fire is abundantly present.
- Watch a fireworks display with a new respect for the power of fire.
- Consider the many ways the element of fire is manifested on our planet.
- Think of as many ways as you can to use fire—actual or metaphoric—in healing. Burning out an illness through fever is a good example.

Burn candles scented with essential oils that are associated with the element of fire. As you inhale the spicy fragrance of fire, try this evocation:

Burning bright, burning higher,
Burning, blazing, golden, fire;
Transform the sick into the well,
Burn away any earthly hell.
Fire my friend and fire my aid.
May a healing tonight be made;
Burn the old so the new can be born,
I praise your heat and you I adorn.

Understanding the Element of Water

Present yourself to the Queen of the Undines and let her know what you are seeking. She may suggest places to go or spirits to visit in her faery world. Or, she might recommend ways you can work with water in your own home. She may wish to speak with you after you've completed your work. Here are some possibilities:

- Think of how many ways water touches your life each day: showers, drinking, rain, washing dishes or clothes, keeping your car engine cool, purifying, etc.
- Contemplate the cleansing and renewing aspect of water. Think about baptisms and other sacred water rites.
- Go to a sacred well. If none exists near you, visit one in faeryland.
- Sit beside a lake, stream, or the ocean.
- Find a large, bowl-shaped stone to hold rain and dew. Consecrate it to the healing powers of the Undine Queen and her faery legions.
- Go swimming and enjoy the sensation of the cool water running over your skin.
- Sit beneath a waterfall or in your shower and allow the water to cleanse you of all negative thoughts.
- Be aware that potable water is endangered. Do your part to keep the water in your community clean. Use water conservatively and conscientiously.
- Dance and sing in the rain.

- Consider how many ways water can be used in healing. Hydrotherapy for relieving arthritis and using cool, damp cloths to soothe a fever are two examples.

Water scents are easy to pick out: They have the heaviness of the ocean and the lightness of the spray that rises from waves. Wear scents that will help connect you to water, such as kelp, moonwort, lily, lotus, and all plants that grow in a watery environment. Try this as an evocation to the element of water:

> *Waves that break high over my head,*
> *I laugh in your spray and play in your bed;*
> *The sand so wet, and the water so cool,*
> *I ask you to be my healing tool.*
> *Water so deep, mysterious shine,*
> *Water and moonlight, essence of divine;*
> *Mold me and make me a healer of all,*
> *Let me stand fast in your breakers tall.*

Sacred Duties and Obligations

The mantle of responsibility you are taking on extends far beyond yourself, or even the people you care about. Becoming a faery shaman—like being any type of shaman—places you in service to others. This is the magickal world's highest calling, but also its most difficult. In this case, you will be exactly what we define a shaman to be: one who walks between worlds, able to work, live, and communicate with beings of many worlds each day—maybe even being able to extend beyond just two worlds if there is a need to be met.

As a faery shaman, you have made a binding contract with the spiritual world to fulfill a role of counselor, healer, seer, and activist for beings living in at least two different worlds. Every shaman's situation is unique, and the unexpected can arise after years of doing your duties without experiencing any emergencies.

In general, these are the duties and obligations you agree to when you accept your faery shaman initiation:

- Once the general population becomes aware you're a healer, you will have more requests than you can handle. Some of these are chronic hypochondriacs, others are poor souls who have not found relief through traditional medical channels. The choice to work with these people or not is up to you, but it is a decision to be made with serious consideration.
- In as far as it is possible for you to control, you will do no harm to anyone in any world for any reason.
- Your shamanic role is one of a healer of body, mind, emotion, and spirit for both humans and faery.
- You accept the help and assistance of the world of nature and the faeries we call nature spirits to help guide you in your healing efforts.
- You must be ready and willing to be called by the nature spirits to heal and to assist them when they are afraid, dying, hurt, or in danger.
- You must do everything to the best of your abilities, both magickally and physically, to bring about the desired outcome in each unique situation. You must never give up until you have exhausted every method of healing and every healing ally you have.
- You are expected to study the human body and its various operating systems, understand how they work, what the most common problems with them are, and what medical doctors and other alternative healers like yourself feel are the best treatments.
- You may have to expose yourself to some danger in your healing efforts. No one expects you to die for their cure, but you will be expected to do your best with what you have.
- You are expected to learn about various ecosystems, how they are endangered, and what you can do to help retrieve and support the environment of Mother Earth.
- You are expected to study herbalism, both magickal and medicinal, and to learn about reactions and interactions.
- You should have an excellent intellectual and experiential knowledge of the major chakras, or energy points, on the body; also what signs of health or illness correspond to each one. The

connections between specific sensory functions and body systems should become as familiar to you as your name.

- You are expected to learn all you can about the world of faery, not just the nature spirits who assist us in healing and in working to save the environment.
- Learn to recognize the different faery species, their habits, customs, likes and dislikes. Many books are available that tell and show the many faces and facets of faery. Some of these books are listed in the Bibliography at the back of this book.
- You should have a functional knowledge of the anatomy of the human body.
- You will be expected to be on call 24/7 if a healing emergency arises in either the human or faery world.
- You will be expected to keep on hand common medicinal herbs and to be well versed in the uses of natural magick.
- You must give the client or faery for whom you are working the same courtesy of confidentiality that a medical doctor must give to his or her patients. Medical records can be copied or given to the client, but anyone else requesting access has to produce a subpoena first.
- You must remain committed to serving in the capacity of a faery shaman, without pretense or arrogance.
- You must not experiment with treatments. If you are unsure how to help someone, then refer that person or faery to someone else with different skills than yours.
- Always remember an adverse or allergic reaction to any substance may occur at any time, even after years and years of it never manifesting.
- Giving respect and doing your duties repays you threefold when you need help.
- Recognize that even the most gifted healers are often beset with afflictions they cannot heal, nor can they find any person or faery who can do more than make the ill person or faery more comfortable.
- You are expected to be humble enough to go to the fey for your own healing needs, recognizing that they have much to teach

you, and you should never behave as if you are higher up on some metaphysical ladder than they.

- Your spiritual self will expand as you do your duties as a faery shaman with love and willingness. What you give will be returned to you threefold at least.
- The results of spiritual contentment should show in your mannerisms, speech, touch, thoughts, and in the way you conduct your life.
- You cannot be "unmade" a faery shaman once you accept that talisman from the world of faery. Only physical death breaks this commitment, at least as far as we know.
- Follow up on clients and faery beings whom you have treated. Even if you've heard from others that they are well, it is courteous and respectful to check on clients for yourself. Do not be surprised if a few faery gifts arrive at your door from time to time.
- Arrange for any healing materials or talisman you have been given by faery to be returned to them or destroyed upon your death. They are not meant to be passed along, not even to one of your own children should that child grow up to be a gifted healer.
- Be sure to offer lavish thanks for such gifts. It is not easy to remove a physical item from one world and transport it into another. If this happens, it is an honor.
- Giving up or ignoring your duties will make further interaction with faery difficult at best, as you will no longer be trusted to keep your word. Faery can be nasty when disrespected or ignored.

If you feel you've passed these basic requirements, and have fulfilled your responsibilities, then you are to be congratulated and commended.

The Healer's Conundrum

One peculiar aspect of becoming a healer that should be given serious thought is that those who become skilled at healing others often lose the ability to heal themselves. It is not unusual for Reiki practitioners to lose the connection to their own illnesses, or for faery shamans to be able to heal everyone but themselves. The famous faery healer of Ireland, Biddy Early, was almost paralyzed by arthritis in her elder years.

No philosopher, clergyperson, or medical doctor can give a reasonable explanation for why this happens. Yet, this phenomenon is visible in many other occult arts, not just faery healing. Tarot card readers often find they can read with stunning accuracy for everyone but themselves. Many psychics cannot see their own futures.

As you continue as a healer, keep notes about your own health, not just your physical body but your emotional and spiritual health as well. Who knows? Maybe you will be the healer who sees a pattern and finally figures out this puzzle.

7

Faery Healing with Plants

As a faery shaman you'll probably use a variety of healing techniques including plant and herbal medicine. Some are safer than others, and I recommend you stick with the safest until you have become skilled in this art. Faery will assist you, which helps cut your risk factor, but even the fey cannot predict what will happen in any individual situation.

When it comes to the specific practice of healing with faery assistance, we work primarily with one race of the faery kingdom: the faeries we know as nature spirits. These are the souls or spirits of a particular plant, herb, flower, or tree. Many nature spirits are bound to the plant they live within, much as our own souls are attached to us and can venture only so far from our host bodies. Only the actual soul of the plant is needed for healing work, and it can be called upon for assistance in most cases.

Transferring Energy

The easiest way to bring faery energy to an ailing person is by transporting a plant that contains faery energy. If you are working with a faery or plant that cannot be moved from its faeryland home, ask if there is another plant you can move instead. Be diplomatic. Faery feelings are easily hurt, and they do not appreciate having their possessions taken away or borrowed without being asked first for their permission.

If you cannot take a faery plant back to the earthly realm to help heal a human patient, ask if the faery would transfer some of his or her healing energy to you. If the faery is willing, allow him or her to put healing energy into your palms, solar plexus, or heart chakra area. If you have an astral "medical kit," you can use that too.

Don't panic. When we refer to things used in the astral plane, we are speaking of things which we have, build, or keep in the astral. For example, some people who astrally project frequently will have a sword or wand waiting for them. Travelers simply take up this object and move about at will and use the "elemental weapons," as they are often called, if and when they are needed. A faery shaman rarely needs this kind of psychic protection.

Your astral medical kit is a bag, case, medicine bag, backpack, or whatever you envision yourself using in the astral world of faery to heal the fey, or in which to store plant energy you need to have for healing others in your own world. Never get the idea that just because something is "only" in your mind that it is not real. Spiritual seekers who make that mistake are humbled with haste. And never get the idea that something you create for yourself in your mind to use in the otherworlds is not real. Occultist have long taught that each mind is a universe unto itself, and what our minds accept to be real and true is what our physical selves believe to be real and true.

You'll find none of this easy, unless you've practiced the astral arts before, but faery will help guide you as you strive to meet your shamanistic goals. You can heal astrally or remotely by appearing with the faeries on the astral plane at the side of the client's bed. From this vantage point the chakras will be visible and you will have a better idea of how to proceed. To move about astrally is to move your consciousness elsewhere. To sustain those visions is at first difficult, but becomes easier with practice. For now, just do it, and don't worry about your wandering mind or the brain chatter trying to tell you this is not possible. Just do it!

The fey will help you administer astral healing. Usually the scenario is, when you are at the bedside of your client, you assess that person's chakras and aura. In other words, their energy centers and the energy surrounding the body. You want it to be bright, free of empty spaces or debris. Do what you can to adjust any imbalances in the chakras and the aura using the faeries as guides.

To extract the debris, use your hands to gather all the healing power you were given by faery, drawing it from your solar plexus or wherever you've stored it until now. Place your palms on the ill person's afflicted area, or on his/her solar plexus if you prefer. Transfer the healing vibrations into your client by visualizing energy flowing from your hands and into the person who needs it. Energy can also be projected from you with thought of healing. Most spiritual speakers know this as "visualization." Keep visualizing healing energy being drawn into you as a gift from faery, and "see" it flow from you into your patient. You may project this energy mentally, through touch, or by any other means which makes you feel the energy passing through you from the faery world to the physical world where someone needs your healing help.

Again, get it out of your head that you are "making it all up" or that it is not "really happening." If you cannot overcome that thinking you will never be a healer or a shaman. At first it will feel fake. We all question our spiritual experiences, which is one of the uniting features of all spiritual paths: Am I right? What you need to ask is: Am I doing right for myself and/or for the person who has asked for my help?

It takes time to trust in yourself and the faery you've partnered with, but the trust will come as will your acceptance of its reality.

When you are done with an astral healing, spend a few minutes watching your patient for signs that the healing is starting to work. Follow up with the client the next morning. You may need to provide more than one treatment. Or, you may need to enlist the assistance of several nature spirits to cure the ailment.

Methods for Healing with Plants and Plant Spirits

Plant and herbal medicine has been practiced by healers, wise men and women, and shamans around the world for centuries. Among the healing methods you may wish to explore are:

- Using dried herbs to make a tea.
- Using warmed herbs to make a poultice for laying upon the skin. Wrap the warm, damp herbs in a clean cloth and place

it on the afflicted area. Poultices were common treatments for colds and flu long before modern antibiotics and antivirals. They are still used to help break up chest congestion.

- Wrapping an injured area with fresh plants. Aloe vera is the most common of these.
- Baking the ingredients into foods.
- Creating a soup using the healing ingredients.
- Making the herb into a paste or ointment; use it directly on skin if it is safe, otherwise use as a poultice.
- A simple infusion of herbs with hot water can be used as a soothing wash or as an alternative to tea. Remove the herbs from the water you have boiled them in and use it as a mild tea.
- Use this same water to put into a soothing bath.
- Keep the healing plant near the ailing person's bed. Introduce the nature spirit to the client and let both know how they can work together to heal.
- Use plants or their essential oils to scent the air. This is called aromatherapy, and it is one of the safer methods of plant medicine.

How to Test for Allergies

Many people are unaware they have allergies. Pharmaceutical companies know there will always be a small subset of the population who will have a dangerous allergic reaction to their medicines. The most modest symptoms can mean something you've ingested or that has come into contact with your skin can be wreaking havoc in your immune system. Foods, medicines, soaps, fabrics, household cleaners, shampoos—virtually any natural or manmade product has the potential to generate an allergic response.

Some of us develop allergies over the years, others grow out of them as our body chemistry changes. Before you use plants, herbs, or any other substance for healing or magickal work, test it to see if you are allergic to it.

The soft inner part of your arm is one of the best test sites. Take some of the plant you wish to use for healing and rub it into the skin. It is best to use the fresh plant. Dried plants—the ones you will most often be using for healing—have lost most of their oils, and it is the oils that most often cause the reaction. Using the fresh plant will allow you to see just how sensitive you are to it. Don't use any plant, fresh or dried, in your healing work if the test indicates a sensitivity.

After applying the plant oil, take a sterile needle and scratch the area gently to make sure the plant is reaching below the top layer of the skin. You can sterilize a needle by heating it in a flame and rubbing off the carbon with a clean cloth and a bit of bleach, or you can buy the sterile lancets diabetics use to test their blood sugar levels. This scratch test introduces an excess of the allergen to the body, probably much more than many medicinal recipes, but it is the quickest and best way to tell if a plant has even the slightest potential of causing a major allergic reaction in you or a client.

Wait twenty-four hours to see if a reaction occurs. Does it itch? Is it red? Is there a welt or hive? Is there a rash? Is the rash spreading? It's possible that an allergic reaction will happen fast, often within a half-hour of contact with the plant. If there is swelling or redness, or if welts appear, rubbing some diphenhydramine cream on the skin can stall the symptoms for a while. (Diphenhydramine is also available over the counter in pill and liquid forms.) Then get immediate medical attention before the allergic reaction worsens. If there is any reaction at all, repeated exposure could result in a full-blown fatal attack of anaphylaxis where the skin swells, hives appear, and the throat closes, restricting breathing.

Keeping Records of Your Healing Work

Record keeping is as essential to your work as a healing faery shaman as it is to any licensed medical doctor. You have no idea when a client is going to come to you with allergic reactions or side effects from an herbal treatment. You need to be able to find this information quickly. If one of your clients has a bad reaction after they leave you, you may be called by a hospital emergency room and asked to identify the substances you used so the correct antidote can be administered.

You also need to keep records showing that you had a long talk with the person who has come to you for healing. You need a full accounting of this person's physical and mental health. Most importantly, you need to be able to note when you referred someone to a licensed medical doctor and have that person sign off that he or she was told to find a licensed medical doctor!

Many people fear seeing a doctor because they don't want to find out how sick they might be. They rationalize that perhaps some friendly advice from the local herbalist will make them feel as they think they should and they can bypass modern medicine. Oddly enough, these same people will gulp down lethal doses of herbs because they are "natural." So is poison ivy, but you don't want it in your stomach. Until you're sure of what you're doing, stick to the astral forms of administering herbs to those who ask for your help.

You also need to keep notes on the things you provide to yourself, such as raspberry tea for cramps or catnip to help you sleep. These will help you see how certain herbs work with the body.

The following questions are ones which should go into all records you keep. Not everyone will tell you everything you would like to know. There are also people who hide health information from their medical doctors. If someone cannot give you enough information for you and your fey helpers to make logical decisions, then you should refer this client to a medical doctor and have him or her sign off on one of these sheets acknowledging that you have taken no action and that you have referred him or her to a licensed medical professional. Retain all pages of the interview with initials and signatures for your legal protection. By law, medical records are the property of the patient. In this case, your "client" should be provided with photocopies of what has transpired.

CLIENT INTERVIEW AND FAERY HEALING CASE RECORD

Day, date, and time of interview

Client's name

Gender

Date of birth

Place of birth

Client's horoscope

Solar zodiac sign

Occupation

Occupational hazards

Avocations

Avocational hazards

Known allergies

Client's home environment

Client's work environment

Has client ever been treated for a chemical imbalance?

If so, when and why?

Client's current spiritual beliefs

Client's family's spiritual beliefs

Element client is most comfortable with

Why client contacted you (in his or her own words)

Client's health history

All medicines and supplements being taken

Client's family health history

Client Interview and Faery Healing Case Record

Current medical, emotional, or spiritual state

What client wants you to do

Does client know faery healing?

Other faery or shamanic treatments tried and discarded

Why they were discarded

Is client currently being treated by a medical professional?

Who and how?

Is client currently using other alternative healing methods?

What and how much?

Does the medical professional know about the alternative therapies client is using? If not, faery shaman must insist that all treatments be disclosed to the medical professional. No exceptions! (Have client initial this to acknowledge that he or she has been asked to fully disclose all treatments to his or her doctor.)

Is client willing to give you access to current medical records?

Would the client like you to accompany him or her to the next doctor appointment?

Overall feelings about what client has told you

Do you believe faery healing can help this person?

Does client give permission for faery healing? (Have client initial here)

Is client going to go on the faery realm journey with you? (Client must have knowledge and skills for this venture)

Day, date, and time of faery journey

Where you were directed in the faery world

What beings greeted you

CLIENT INTERVIEW AND FAERY HEALING CASE RECORD

What beings spoke to you

Did a particular element seem to be extending itself to you?

Did you make your intent for being in this part of the faery realm known?

Describe how you were taken or led

Describe who or what took you or led you

Describe where you were taken or led

Were words or images of healing instructions given to you?

Did specific plant or plants call for your attention?

Did any being suggest that the client needed medical help in addition to faery healing or in place of faery healing? (They know what they can and cannot do; respect it.)

Describe the rest of the healing quest

If patient did not do a joint shamanic journey with you did you relate all of your journey? You must!

If patient went along, what are his or her impressions and memories?

Will faery healing be done?

Describe in detail the faery healing—the method, how much, how long, by whom, etc.?

Have client sign off that all that has been encountered will be reported to his or her doctor.

Date client's case closed

Reason for termination

Final Action: Client acknowledges you are not a licensed physician, nor are you intending to take the place of one.

Have him or her sign, then print name and date for this interview.

Resources for Safe Herb Selection

Safety first is a good axiom to follow when using herbs and plants for healing purposes, whether the "patient" is human or faery. Each species has its own unique makeup that will affect how illness and healing occur. What is good for faery might not be good for humans, and vice versa. Additionally, some diseases that we succumb to might not be dangerous to faeries, whereas some faery ailments might not impact us at all.

Some diseases can be passed between faery and humans. In some cases, the severity of the reaction may be due to lack of immunity— remember what happened when Europeans first came to the New World and infected the native population with contagions they'd never been exposed to before.

Faery Alert

Do not risk picking a plant for medical use unless you are 100 percent sure of its identity, even if its spirit is telling you to go for it. Just because it's natural doesn't mean it's safe. You're in a partnership with faery, and they will help you, but they have knowledge gaps about humans just as we do about them. Would you know what herbal tea to give a house Brownie with the flu? Would you know the plant on sight? Probably not. If you are uncertain about a particular plant's properties, ask your local health food store or herbal shop to recommend an expert.

Many herbs are available via mail. Appendix A in the back of this book contains URLs for sites that sell nature remedies, herbs, and other items needed to make your own medicines. Before you start using them, however, it's wise to read some good books on the subject and/or take some classes in herbal medicine. There are also lots of books about working with faery for healing. Here are some that have been of the greatest help to me.

My friend and colleague, Margie McArthur, devotes an entire chapter in her book, *Faery Healing: The Lore and the Legacy* (Aptos, CA: New Brighton Books, 2003), to diseases we may contract from the fey and how to treat them. She writes about the most common faery ailments we are susceptible to. Interestingly, one is the freedom and joy we feel in the faery realm. Folklore from all over the world tells of humans who have spent time in the world of faery and pined for it so much that they died from the wanting, just as some people die of broken hearts.

Scott Cunningham's *Cunningham's Encyclopedia of Magical Herbs* is a classic text among magickal people.

Another excellent resource is *Plant Spirit Shamanism*, by Ross Heaven and Howard G. Charing (Rochester, VT: Destiny Books, 2006). It is somewhat controversial because it includes hallucinogenic plants, but you should have a working knowledge of these whether you choose to use them or not. If you are not Pagan, you will find this book is written in language more familiar to you than other books on plant shamanism.

Nature-Speak: Signs, Omens & Messages in Nature, by Ted Andrews (Jackson, TN: Dragonhawk Publishing, 2004) does for plant totems what his book *Animal Speak* did for the study of totem animals. It is a good place to start learning what the spirit of each tree, flower, or herb is trying to tell you.

There are also sources to learn about herbs online, but please be careful with these. You have no idea if the person posting the information has gleaned it from personal experience, other sources (which may or may not be correct), or if the anonymous webmeister is just making things up as he or she goes along. I have listed a few sites I think are very good in Appendix A of this book. These do not represent all of the sites that provide solid information, they are just ones I have visited frequently and, so far, everything they've said has been accurate.

The Magickal Art of Faery Aromatherapy

It is astounding the changes that can result from something as simple as choosing what you breathe. In recent years, aromatherapy has become mainstream—aromatherapy candles and oils are now sold in supermarkets and pharmacies. Some scents invigorate, some calm stress, some lift the spirits, some spark intuition or imagination. Using pure essential oils—not synthetic fragrances—sparingly in your environment works best.

Burning incense is another form of aromatherapy. If you buy joss stick or cone incenses, make sure you have high-quality products. You want the herb to be the ingredient that comes first or second on the list.

Use incense coals, never the charcoal briquettes designed for cooking outdoors, to burn loose incense, dried herbs, or resins. Cooking charcoals contain chemicals that are toxic in confined areas.

This is a list of some popular aromatic fragrances. Those derived from plants that are said by folklore to be faery favorites are followed by an asterisk.

Invigorating Scents

- Bay
- Cedar
- Cinnamon
- Lemon
- Lemongrass
- Mint
- Myrtle *
- Rosemary
- Soothing Scents
- Apple Blossom
- Frankincense
- Heather *
- Honeysuckle *
- Hyssop
- Jasmine
- Lavender *
- Lilac
- Lotus
- Magnolia
- Orange Blossom
- Patchouli

Oils best used as tools for healing are known as aromatherapy. Though this art was being used as early as 5,000 years ago in the Middle East, its use has become mainstream with scented oils and air sprays being pitched on daily television. As the shaman you are the conduit between worlds. Your connection to an oil's energy by scent or touch will transfer the healing energy from faery to physical.

Oils that are not caustic, and will not cause an allergic reaction on the patient—which requires some planning ahead—can be carefully placed on the chakra points, or body energy centers:

1. Root Chakra, red in color at the base of the tailbone
2. Navel Chakra, orange in color just beneath your belly button
3. Solar Plexus Chakra, yellow in color and located in the soft area beneath your breastbone
4. Heart Center Chakra, green in color and between your breasts at the level of your heart
5. Throat Chakra, blue in color and found in the small hollow at the base of your throat
6. Third-Eye Chakra, blue-violet in color and found just between and above your eyes
7. Crown Chakra, violet or white in color and located just above the crown of your head

I will caution the new shaman about confusing the oil properties of a herb, plant, or flower, with the energies or known properties of the botanical itself. Some plant parts are benign while others are toxic. Many faery scents can be toxic or even deadly when inhaled, ingested, or placed on the skin. Skin eruptions are probably the single most common adverse reaction to an essential oil. Keep them diluted and never ingest them!

For anything more detailed than basic treatments for common conditions, you will have to go to faery and seek your own cures. In the beginning try cross-checking your faery information with that found in books on medicinal aromatherapy. Some oils are dangerous even to breathe, and they can scar the lungs and burn mucus membranes. Remember, you are a student shaman, not a licensed physician. You probably don't have an advanced degree in botany either. Err on the side of caution and use visualized energies of the oils you smell rather than the oil itself. Make the transfer to the patient as you were told to earlier in this chapter.

The following herbs should NEVER be used in an incense. I've included them here for informational purposes only. Artificial versions of many of these poison plants are available, but an incense made out of chemical compounds engineered to smell like the real thing will not work at the vibrational rate you need. Also, remember that anyone can have or develop an allergy to a substance, natural or not. If anyone shows signs of breathing distress, douse the incense with water and seek immediate medical help. If a plant is one you would not eat, don't try to make it into a medicine for someone else to eat. You are a beginner in this art and you don't want to learn all your lessons the hard way—at the expense of someone else's life and health.

- Bluebell
- Broom
- Foxglove
- Lily of the Valley
- Nettles
- Oleander
- Poppy
- Poison Ivy or Oak
- Ragweed
- Toadstool
- Any substance to which your client tells you he or she is allergic

These precautions are not meant to scare anyone away from pursuing faery shamanism, but they are here to make you overcautious in your work, especially when it is new to you. The best rule to heal by: If you're not 100 percent sure of the outcome, don't use it physically. There is always the astral plane to experiment with energies of which you are unsure. You must also be ethical with your patient and explain any possible pros and cons to him or her. You work for the patient, not the other way around. If a patient says no to a specific treatment you *do not* give it, no matter how much you may think you're doing it for their own good. This is malpractice in the shaman's world.

The Concept of Vibration

A lot of New Age books talk about vibration or vibrational levels. The truth is that there is nothing "new" about these concepts. It is a very old belief that is essential to understand if you're going to be an effective faery healer. Once again, we have semantics in our way. This is a concept no harder to grasp than that of the astral world or of the nonphysical energy of plants.

Let's start with the basics.

Everything everywhere is made up of molecules, and all molecules vibrate. They are made up of smaller atoms which give a charge or a life to the molecule to which they are chemically bound. The distance between the molecules decides the density of an object. For example, the molecules of an old oak tree move very little because the material they are binding together is dense. Water is less dense, therefore its molecules move more. Get this in your head and you have a basic picture of how the universe—both the seen and the unseen parts—is put together.

In metaphysics it is considered good to have high vibrations as opposed to low ones. High vibrations send off a positive charge, and low vibrations send off a negative charge. In metaphysics like attracts like, so, in order to attract the faeries of highest good, you want to have a high vibration in both your physical and astral bodies.

An object's physical density has nothing to do with the quality of its molecular vibrations. An old oak tree can vibrate at a high level even though its molecules are bound too tightly to allow movement to be seen by the naked eye. Oak has been a sacred tree in many cultures. The wood is hard and strong. It grows from small acorns, and lives a long life, often hosting other healing plants such as mistletoe. The oak vibrates at a high rate spiritually because of these properties.

By the same logic we can conclude that molecules with a looser bond, such as water, do not necessarily have a higher spiritual vibration simply because water molecules are not so tightly bound. Polluted or stagnant water produces a much lower vibration than fresh spring water.

Compare this to the health of a human being. When we feel good, mentally and physically, it shows. There is a bounce in our step, we smile with ease, we are more receptive to people around us. Those positive energies cause our molecules to vibrate at a higher rate than they do when we are depressed or angry.

How Do Molecular Vibrations Work?

We must understand that we are all made of molecules, and that the density of our physical bodies has no relation to our spiritual vibrations. The former comes from the natural laws of the universe, the latter is what we seek to attain and retain.

Experience is wisdom, so try to experience these two examples of human body vibrations as I relate them. Let's take the example of a concrete wall and a wind tunnel. There you are, facing the concrete wall. Can you physically pass through that wall? Of course not. Your molecules are not as dense as those of the wall. You would have to vibrate yourself into invisible pieces to make your molecular structure fit between those of the wall. Those molecules are vibrating too, but there are more of them, and they stay close together no matter how high their vibrational rate.

In the wind tunnel you can practically feel the air pass right through you, just as it does on a blustery winter's day. The molecules of air are not only vibrating, they are in motion mode. They are small enough to actually enter your body, to pass right through the molecular structure that makes up your body. You feel your lungs struggle to keep you breathing and your heart rate may rise with the effort of moving against the wind. The molecular structure of the wind is less dense and vibrating faster than that of your body.

You also have your astral body or your consciousness, and it is that part of you which must vibrate with a high spiritual energy to allow you access to the healing world of the fey and other spiritual worlds. Close your eyes and center yourself. Allow the image of a concrete wall come to mind. Imagine that there is something important on the other side that you need to have to heal someone. Now take your astral self through the wall. You are no longer blocked by molecular differences, but rather, because both you and the wall hide things of good and positive intent, you pass through one another with ease.

The same is true of the wind tunnel. Begin to visualize again. Let the gale forces come at you as you visualize a patient who needs your help who lies just beyond the gale. Once again, your spiritual vibrations will allow you and the wind to pass through one another for a common and positive spiritual goal.

The Right Degree of Vibration for Faery Healing

It is not advisable to perform healings or other spiritual work when you are not feeling your best. When you are sick or tired, your vibration rate drops. On the astral plane like energies attract. They also determine which areas of the astral world are open to you. If you are ill, frustrated, tired, depressed, or angry, you will enter the astral place with a low vibration rate, one that draws to you denizens of the otherworlds who are vibrating at a low rate. They feed off your store of energy, leaving you sucked dry.

As faery shamans we are able to get inside the realm of the nature spirits because we create a vibrational rate within ourselves that corresponds to or is higher than that of the nature spirits' world. If our vibrations were lower we could not enter that environment. In this state we meld easily with the otherworlds that eventually ascend to the realm of the deities.

This process is harder to explain than it is to understand. One thing that can catapult both you and any beings immediately surrounding you to the right rate of vibration is burning incense. The incenses listed below are known to help change the vibrational atmosphere where they are burned. Many faeries do not like smoke—it drives them away like mosquitoes—but many other plant faery spirits tolerate smoke for the uplifting effect it has on us and on them when placed in an incense formula to accomplish a healing. When we are both vibrating to the same rhythm, coming together to work and play as one is just easier to accomplish, and it is easier for us to change our ways than for faery.

Some Scents That Affect Vibration

Below is a list of scents that please the fey. I've also noted which ones can aid dreaming, divination, and dream magick. All of these will assist in raising the spiritual vibrations in the area in which it is used. Feel free to combine scents if you feel moved to or if a faery healing partner makes the suggestion.

- Apple Blossom
- Columbine
- Cowslip (also called Faery Cup—use a synthetic in this case)
- Daffodil

- Daisy (good for divination dreams)
- Dogwood (a faery scent that is very hard to find)
- Gardenia (helps inspire dreams of healing)
- Grass (natural prairie or pasture grasses are best)
- Hawthorn (sacred to many faeries)
- Honesty (a synthetic is recommended)
- Honeysuckle
- Hyssop
- Iris
- Jasmine (excellent for encouraging prophetic dreams)
- Lavender (opens your dreams to love and to otherworld secrets)
- Lemon Verbena (helps produce dreams of prophecy)
- Lilac (promotes dreams of past lives)
- Magnolia
- Marigold
- Mullein (seeds are poison, use a prefabricated joss stick or cone instead)
- Orange Blossom (brings dreams of a future mate)
- Pansy
- Passion Flower
- Poppy (a synthetic is recommended)
- Petunia (helps restore memory of things forgotten)
- Primrose (can induce sexual dreams and draw to you a faery lover)
- Raspberry
- Red Clover (good for dreams of prosperity)
- Rose (all colors)
- Rosemary (not most favored by the fey, but useful in all dream needs)
- Rue
- Snapdragon
- Strawberry
- Sunflower
- Vervain
- Violet
- White Clover (offers protection during dream journeys)
- Yellow Evening Primrose (helps prevent nightmares)

8

Other Faery Healing Techniques

Although a significant part of your faery healing work will most likely involve the use of herbs, flowers, and other plants, as a faery shaman you'll want to explore some of the other magickal healing practices available to you. These techniques may sound a bit strange to people who aren't familiar with faery or with magick in general. But don't let that put you off. The methods discussed in this chapter can be very powerful and effective.

Elemental Faery Magick for Wholeness and Well-Being

We've already discussed the elemental rulers—the Gnome King, the Salamander King, the Undine Queen, and the Sylph Queen—and the huge influence they have in the kingdoms they oversee. By asking their help in our life choices we can help balance elemental energies in our bodies and minds, to promote wholeness and well-being.

There is a reason even the most confirmed city dweller experiences emotional renewal from a weekend in the great outdoors. Quite simply, exposure to nature and the elements fills the empty spots in us, making us more complete and functioning beings.

The elements are to our spiritual, mental, and emotional bodies what red blood cells and a strong immune system are to our physical bodies. Sometimes we need to ground ourselves in the healing energies of one particular element for a while until we feel it sealing up those holes. This renewal can be as simple as just knowing we need to leave the "asphalt jungle" behind periodically and revel in the elements for a while.

We have no idea how old the concepts of elements and elemental rulers are, but they must have been strong archetypes in the human mind because when it came to deciding what the basic building blocks that made up everything in the universe were, ancient people seemed to find much in common. In Western Europe and Euro-North America we tend to use four elements: earth, air, fire, and water, but we also bring in the element of spirit, which unites the others. Earth and water seem to be universal, but some cultures consider wood or metal as separate elements; others recognize as many as five or seven elements.

Faery Tales

"My definition of Faery Healing is this: Accessing the regenerative and healing powers of the Otherworlds—the Faery Realm, and by extension, the powers of the Elemental and Divic realms, as well as that of the Deep Earth—for purposes of healing work, which is the work of 'reconnecting and reweaving into wholeness.'" —Margie McArthur, *Faery Healing: The Lore and the Legacy*

You can discover which element(s) you lack by looking at your horoscope (or birth chart). Few charts are balanced in all four elements; most are weighted toward one or two elements, and might not even contain a single feature in one element.

Most people are familiar with "sun sign" astrology, which considers only the zodiac sign the sun was in when you were born. We identify with our sun signs. When you say, "I am a Libra," for instance, you are making a statement that says something about your outer personality. Although astrology is much more complex than this, for the purposes of this chapter we'll only consider the sun signs and their elemental groupings.

Each of the twelve signs of the zodiac falls into one or another of the elements: earth, air, fire, and water. Each element embodies certain characteristics that you'll display if your sun (or other astrological features) falls into that element. If nothing in your chart corresponds to a particular element, you won't really understand the nature of that energy and may need some assistance to balance the weakness.

Earth Signs: Taurus, Virgo, Capricorn

Earth Traits: Solid, dependable, loves nature, has a green thumb, but he can be stubborn. Earth enjoys teamwork, but prefers to take charge of a project. Detail-oriented, he thrives on living up to his responsibilities and doing the best job he can. Earth signs are usually kind and friendly, though sometimes shy.

Air Signs: Gemini, Libra, Aquarius

Air Traits: Intellectual, sociable, given to wanderlust. Air has to know why and how things work, and searches constantly for universal truths. She enjoys teamwork as long as she is clear about her place in the team. She detests laziness, thinks things through before acting, but can be as capricious as the wind. She also enjoys intellectual debates and all types of communication.

Fire Signs: Aries, Leo, Sagittarius

Fire Traits: Outgoing, adventurous, self-motivated, life of the party. Fire people must consider changes with care—when fire is ready it burns down the old to create the new. They like the limelight, want to be center stage; they need to be liked and to feel special. Fire can have a commanding royal attitude, or be sweet as a kitten. They try to play to the weaknesses of others rather than start a confrontation, but rarely back down from an opponent.

Water Signs: Cancer, Scorpio, Pisces

Water Traits: Intuitive, moody, introverted. Water loves home, family, and children. They can be emotionally unpredictable and secretive as the ocean. These sensitive people experience the world through feelings. Although she may waffle initially, once a water sign makes up her mind she rarely turns back. Water prefers close relationships with one or two special people than groups of friends.

You have probably noticed discrepancies in your birth sign element and in your personality. This is because our sun signs do not tell our whole story—sometimes the complete birth chart does not answer all the questions we have about ourselves. It's a wonderful starting point, however, and you may choose to have your chart calculated by an astrologer to see which elements are strong or weak in you.

Where and how you live also influences your elemental balance. If you live in the desert where opening your front door feels like opening a blast furnace, you may have too much fire in your psyche. If you live in Seattle, the water element may overwhelm you.

Our elements were to magickal people of the past, and to many modern seekers, what the Periodic Table of Elements is to modern science. They represent the smallest component found in all things, around which all else must be built.

The Faery Dream Spell: the Element of Water

Dreams are powerful. One with vivid imagery or that deals with current problems the dreamer is having during waking hours can be immediately helpful.

The elemental rulers of water are the Undines, and, with their help, you can induce a dream in anyone's head which will help them seek their own cures or find their own way to faery. You want to plant the seed of knowledge in the dreamer's head so he or she can solve problems on their own. Using water and dream incubation techniques, it is possible to induce a dream in another person that will be remembered for its clarity and cherished for the pathway it opened.

To begin you will need to find water from a natural place. It might not be clean water, but it is not for consumption, nor will it be placed on broken skin.

Stir your bowl of water with a water-ruled tree branch or other plant that offers itself. I'm partial to using a bit of willow branch when the fey give me permission to take one. Otherwise I look on the ground and hope to find one already separated from the willow.

Have the person seeking treatment lie in bed on his or her back to begin the healing dream induction. Stir the water bowl clockwise to begin. You are raising energy for the dream spell:

> Queen of the Undines, and her subjects of the deep,
> Bless _____ (name of person to be healed) with a restful sleep;
> In your watery world between dark and light,
> Guide her way to wellness through a clear dream tonight.

Take the willow branch or other item and use it to gently anoint the chakra points with a small bit of the water. Dip the branch or other item back into the water in the bowl between each chakra, starting from the root and moving on up to the crown chakra.

Now stir counterclockwise to release the dream energies you've created. Chant your client into a light sleep with a simple sentence that sums up the problem and asks for a solution. Don't sweat over this. It doesn't need to be more than a single sentence, and it does not have to rhyme. It is best to chant it rhythmically, but let it come naturally to you. Trust yourself and the magick. Place the damp willow branch or other item near the sleeping person. When he or she awakes holding this to the forehead can help make the dream more memorable.

Be sure to thank the Undines for their assistance before you leave the bedside.

The Faery Transformation Spell: The Element of Fire

Fire is the ultimate element of transformation. It can burn away illness, change our thinking, and even cause change in those around us. Have the person to be healed sit in a natural place, or on his or her own bed. This spell is best done outdoors around foliage that is too damp to be flammable. Fire transforms all it touches, and it moves fast. Use caution and common sense with fire. Never leave a fire unattended. If you cannot be alert until it burns itself out, then you must extinguish the flame yourself.

Use a candle in a color to represent the goal of the spell. There are suggestions as to which color goes with what goal, but, ultimately, it is your choice to make. Blue and purple represent physical or emotional healing. Yellow is used for intellect or willpower. Red burns hot when used with fire to make the element stronger. Orange and gold represent attraction, silver and white for the spiritual self. Green is for prosperity and beauty, and silver is for things unseen.

If you choose a candle, please place it inside a small paper cup with a hole in the bottom to hold it in place. Your client will not be well served by being doused with hot wax.

Taking the fire with you, walk nine times around the client moving counterclockwise. Repeat a simple chant that refers to what the client wishes to change. This is what you will burn off him or her before you open the pathway to transformation. For example, if the client wants to rid themselves of a bad habit, your chant will sound something like this:

> _____ *(name of person to be healed) is a nail biter,*
> *She needs to be a nail bite fighter.*

As you walk and chant, visualize the bad habit and urges that might provoke it, burning off the client and grounding itself harmlessly in Mother Earth.

If you feel the fire has not burned off all the residue you should keep walking, but in silence. When you feel it is time to transform the bad habit into something positive, begin walking at least nine times around your client clockwise:

> _____ *(name of person to be healed) is strong and right,*
> *No more her nails will she bite;*
> *Salamander King and your fire drakes, please,*
> *Heal _____ (name of person to be healed),*
> *Of this self-inflicted disease.*

Again, if you feel the fire is still at work, keep walking, but in silence. When you feel the job is done, thank the Salamanders for their help and, if possible, put out the fire of the candle by turning it upside down and grounding it in Mother Earth. Use caution so that you will not harm other plants or start a fire by doing this. If you cannot do this, then douse the fire with something else that cuts off its oxygen supply.

The Faery Hearing Spell: The Element of Air

The element of air rules communication and areas of intellectual concern. The Sylph Queen and her subjects can be called up to heal forgetfulness in the face of an upcoming exam or when communication must be clear and definite. This is why this spell focuses on hearing. More than speaking, hearing is necessary for clarity, and this means hearing for yourself and to whomever you're speaking.

This spell is best done outside. Note the direction from where the breeze blows. If it is from the east, you are in the native home of the sylphs, and your spell will be better received. If it is not from the east, work with what you have. You might be surprised as the spell progresses that the breeze changes direction for you.

This spell can be done anywhere, even in front of an open window. You will need only a cape, small sheet, scarf, shawl, or some other piece of lightweight fabric that will billow in the wind. A small bit of powdered rosemary is useful to have, but not essential.

Begin dancing with the scarf in front of the window or outside in the open air. Allow yourself to feel at one with the sylphs. As you start to feel a connection you can begin to hum. Just a single measure of melody is all you need. Wait until you begin to hear your notes echoing back to you.

Continue your dance and—depending on your precise goal—is chant something like this over and over:

> Hail, Queen of the Sylphs, and her subjects too,
> Grant to me perfect communication true;
> Help me to listen and to know when to hush,
> Your blesséd breeze through my soul does rush.

If you feel the chant makes you want to sing, then take off and do it. Shaman song is one of the primary skills of a faery shaman. You cannot go wrong by following your intuition in this spell.

When you feel you have danced the air element into yourself, pause, close your eyes, and feel yourself centered and balanced on the ground beneath you. Thank the Queen of the Sylphs and her court for their assistance.

If you have powdered rosemary on hand, blow it into the wind. Rosemary is an herb with many magickal and medicinal uses. As you watch it fly from your open palm, visualize yourself achieving what you set out to gain from this spell.

The Faery Balancing Spell: The Element of Earth

Being in balance as a human being means a lot of systems, including the seen and the unseen, must be in harmony with one another. This alone is healing to the body and spirit. It can also balance out emotions. The element of earth is sturdy and stable, ruled by the Gnome King who lives in the heart of Mother Earth.

For this spell it is best to lie flat on the ground. Grass, a garden, or anywhere in nature where you can feel safe enough to allow your consciousness to fully relax. The relaxation is more important than the locale, so use your home if you must. Hardwood flooring is preferable to carpet. Try to make your area as natural as possible.

When we seek balance we seek to balance all the systems of our bodies with all the others. This not only includes your chakras and physical body, but also your mental, spiritual, and emotional bodies. When you're in balance you can work better as a shaman, think more clearly as a student, let small annoyances roll away from you, and pave the way for a healthier physical body. You can also guide others through the ritual spell to attain the same sense of balance you will achieve.

You are ready to begin when you are comfortable and know you can remain that way for at least thirty minutes.

Call upon the Gnome King and his subjects to assist you in your work. Invite, do not command. They will come.

Begin to let your conscious mind slow, carrying you into receptive levels of activity. Focus only on the Gnomes you've asked to help you. Sense them forming a ring around you and their king. You may feel a tingling or a sense of warmth. You may even hear gnome voices, gentle and low. Imagine yourself sinking into Mother Earth's welcoming arms.

Lie in peace while the Gnome King makes his assessment of any ailments you might not be aware of having, and allow him time to work his magick on those. At some point soon after this you may be aware of a humming noise. That is the vibrations of gnome voices seeking for the musical pitch which will help you balance all your systems.

Tell the Gnome King exactly what you want:

> *King of the Gnomes, on you I call,*
> *So I can be in balance, my all in all;*
> *Body, spirit, emotion, and mind,*
> *In myself must be well combined.*
> *To your magick I open myself,*
> *Praise and thanks to you, Highness of Elfs* (Elves does not
> rhyme, so poor grammar can be excused in these cases)*;*
> *Balance, center, and give healing to me,*
> *As I desire, so mote it be!*

You will feel your chakra areas burst open one by one, starting from the root up. This may tickle or feel hot or cool to you. Accept what it is and continue to lie still. If you have a good psychic eye, your mind will see what is taking place, and most people are comfortable having this sight. If you do not have it yet, keep practicing. One day it will just come. It will be there, and you will be so stunned and ecstatic that you will yank your consciousness out of its receptive state for a while. This is normal and it offends no one. Just start once again with the asking for balance.

You will know when it is time to bring your consciousness back and open your eyes. You will feel recharged, almost like you've had a long, restful night's sleep.

Be sure to thank the gnomes before you leave the area. It is also traditional to offer the gnomes a shiny coin—dimes are a popular gift—a sparkling stone, or some food for the woodland animals cared for by the gnomes.

You will know when it is time to be rebalanced again. As you grow in your shaman's skills you will find you can keep yourself balanced for longer periods of time.

Making and Using Your Own Seguro

Seguro is a Spanish word meaning safe or sure. Faery seers use the word to refer to a tool, sent to a specific shaman from the faery world, that takes the faery shaman into the world of visions. Seguro may be a Spanish word, but its concept as a healing tool is also part of Western European folklore.

Faery Tales

Over a century ago in Ireland lived a woman named Biddy Early. This elderly rural woman was gifted with a blue glass bottle from the faeries—a seguro. When neighbors came for her healing help, she would peer into the bottle, get the right diagnosis, and be told what herb, plant, tea, or ritual was needed to heal those people. Her fame spread, and soon people from all over Ireland migrated to Biddy Early's door to ask for her services. As she continued to heal more and more people of diseases no doctor at that time could manage, her own health deteriorated. She was plagued with rheumatoid arthritis for the last half of her life. Today the blue bottle is said to lie at the bottom of the lake near her home. From time to time divers have searched vainly for it, but it is either buried in the silt at the lake bottom, or has been reclaimed by the faeries.

Using a Seguro as a Faery Shaman's Talisman

Most regular adventurers in the world of faery are eventually given some gift, which may either help in healing, diagnosing, or by offering safe passages throughout the otherworlds. Until such a gift is presented, a simple bottle oracle known as the seguro—made with thought and care with your own hands—can fulfill this role.

The seguro also has roots in Afro-Latin American syncretic religious practices where the bottle is not just a diagnostic tool, but also a spirit ally. In Latin America, and in some Caribbean spiritual practices, these healing bottles are created by the faery shamans themselves. The bottles contain specific plant or herbal totems who help the shamans focus attention on a cure for an ailment. This is a tool for diagnosing and treating illness almost identical to that given to Biddy Early.

A shaman might use one seguro for an entire lifetime, or might have several he or she consults depending on the situation. Some shamans will add to a seguro over time, or they will sometimes reconstruct the seguro from the same bottle so as not to disturb the vibrations the bottle has absorbed that have worked well for so long. With use, and with each item added to the seguro, it begins to shape its own personality, eventually creating its own spirit.

The seguro is also a source of faery-speak. Many alternative healers in Brazil, where the use of seguros is prominent, say they hear voices coming from their bottles. My bottle likes to make groaner puns, usually when I'm taking myself and my issues too seriously.

Some say the shaman who uses the seguro will learn a song that only he or she can sing to summon greater healing power and connect more deeply with faery. The seguro will launch you into discovering other magickal melodies, too. Song magick, as you'll soon learn, is an essential part of shamanic work with faeries. My seguro has never said anything to me that was wrong, so I pay attention when it sings to me.

How to Make Your Own Seguro

As you develop a deeper healing partnership with faery, you can experiment with making your own seguro. You will first need a nice apothecary jar. It should be made of glass, in a shape and style you like, have a corked, wire-sealed, or glass stopper lid, and be big enough to peer into or listen to when held up to your ear. In Latin America clear jars are often used, but I prefer to cloak my personal mysteries behind colored glass like Biddy Early, who received her blue seguro bottle from faery.

You can reuse a dark glass jar that previously held food or beverage, but wash off the labeling and give it a good cleansing before creating a seguro. Metal and rubber lids should be discarded—if you are using essential oils in your bottle they may come into contact with the rubber or metal; rubber will be broken down by the oils and metal will corrode. Once you have found a bottle you feel matches you in temperament and energy, clear the bottle of any existent energies it may carry, either from its former contents or from previous owners. The older your jar, the more cleansing it will need.

Rinse it with lots and lots of water (from the tap or a nearby stream). As you rinse the bottle, visualize the old energies the bottle has collected being washed away. When you feel the bottle has been cleared of all previous energies, keep rinsing it in the water as you run your hands over the glass, imbuing it with your personal energies and healing wishes.

You may feel an urge to hum. This may be your seguro's "soul song." The seguro is going to be a very real and unique personality. Get to know it as well as possible. You will want to learn the bottle's melody, for it will be a healing partner to you second only in importance to faery. In fact, faery will inspire what goes into your personal seguro.

Faery Alert

Only you and the faeries you are working with in developing your healing skills should know what goes into your seguro.

When you feel you and the seguro have merged your energies, dry it off, and allow it to sit out so the inside can dry, too. Each day spend some time holding and fondling the seguro. Hum its song again if you think you hear it. As you do this, keep your mind focused on the goal of this magickal entity you are creating: a seguro to help you in your healing work.

Meditate with the seguro resting on one of your chakra areas. Visualize the relationship you and the bottle will have. Your seguro is

- Your healing partner;
- A way for the fey to communicate with you;
- A source of healing and/or faery song;
- A friend who keeps your secrets;
- An ally who checks your fear;
- A source of knowledge when all other means fail.

As the days pass, start thinking about what you want to put in your seguro. Begin to collect natural objects that resonate with you and that you feel would enhance your healing powers. What and how much you put in is up to you. It is best to be able to see light coming through the glass at some point, so don't fill it completely. You really only need a small amount of each item, enough so that the total mixture covers the bottom of the bottle. You can always add new items later, or empty it and start over.

The basics of the seguro are ashes or salt, oil, and plants or herbs. Ashes and salt are used for grounding, and they will keep the healing images and words that come to you inside the bottle, always available to you. They also keep your soul and that of the seguro rooted in the earth mother. Ashes and salt are also items with protective energy, used for this purpose by magickal people for centuries.

The herbs and/or plants you add will be communicated to you by faery. Go into faeryland to visit one of the elemental rulers or other nature spirits you have befriended. Nature spirits seem to have an instinctive knowledge about what they cannot provide, or if providing them to a specific faery shaman at a specific time is not right. They can also direct you to other plants you may wish to speak with before you begin putting herbs and plant materials in the seguro.

If your forte is emotional healing, you might include water-related or water-grown herbs and plants. An essential oil or some rainwater or natural spring water might be suggested. You should only use minute amounts of each—it doesn't take much to capture the energy. Or, faery may recognize a place where your skills are weak and suggest a plant that will help you fill the gap. Faery may give you all you need to know in one trip, or they may instruct you to go out into the natural world and seek the recommended items. Follow their instructions. They recognize the seguro as a sacred healing object. The fact that you are going to so much trouble to make one shows you are a committed faery shaman, and they will respect that.

After you have gathered all the items to go into your seguro, spread them on a flat surface around the bottle. With your eyes moving clockwise around the circle, say out loud what each item's function will be. On your second pass around the circle, ask each item if it is willing to fulfill its role. If you feel a negative answer, set that item aside. On your third pass around the circle, place each item into the seguro. State aloud what its function is, emphasizing the healing partnership between you, the seguro, and faery.

When you have your seguro complete, cap it. You will only peer into it or hold it to your ear when you need guidance for healing.

When you feel your seguro is ready to serve your current needs, dedicate it to the deities of healing and to your partnership with the healing spirits of nature. Hold the seguro up to the sky and consecrate it by saying:

> *Behold! Ancestors, deities, spirit guides, and fey,*
> *I hold aloft my seguro today;*
> *Bless it with insight, bless it with power,*
> *My partner in healing as of today, this hour.*

Next, hold your seguro against Mother Earth and consecrate it by saying:

> *Earth mother, bless this partner of mine,*
> *A seguro strong, with ingredients fine;*
> *Help me to hear, help me to see,*
> *All that you expect of me.*

Hold the seguro out toward the faeries and consecrate again by saying:

By faeries of day and faeries of night,
Grant to me your healing sight;
To heal show me what I need to know,
Help me as a faery shaman to grow.

Lastly, hold the seguro close to yourself, preferably against the bare skin of your solar plexus, and say:

I consecrate this seguro to healing tasks,
I promise to listen and do what it asks;
I promise to heed what I see inside,
And as my partner it shall abide.
From me, from faery, and back again,
The power of my seguro never can end;
By powers of faery this spell is sealed,
All who ask me shall be healed.
By earth, water, air, and fire,
Which bring me what I desire;
And by the power of three times three,
By my will, so mote it be!

You may sense faery beings closing in around you to add their blessings to your bottle. Do not be scared away by this press of their energy. Unless you have a definite feeling of something unwelcome (which is unlikely), allow faery to enjoy and admire your new healing tool as much as you do.

While you are focused on the higher vibration work of healing, you and the seguro are vibrating too fast for lower, slower entities and energies to slip in between. With this talisman visible fewer trickster spirits and gaming faeries will try to divert your attention from your work. They know our mutual survival depends on the cooperation of the faery shamans.

To use your seguro, take it with you into faeryland. Or, simply pick it up and ask it what you want to know about a healing issue. The seguro may speak, give you a visual imprint, or sing a healing song. If you are uncertain what it is telling you to do, keep asking questions until the meaning is clear. The seguro has eternal patience, and the longer you work together, the better partners you will be.

Though the talisman will always be visible on the etheric planes, to wear a representation of it on the earth plane allows the healing faeries living between the world of faery and the world of humans to recognize you. If you're in a garden, woodland, or near a cave or seashore, and you clearly hear your name spoken, listen. The faeries have a message for you or know where you can find the answer you seek for the healing work you are preparing to do.

Wherever you take your seguro, its energy will resonate with all nature spirits. You might be surprised when the hedge outside your front door says good morning to you someday. What you wear is a sign of trust, an honor you earned during your initiation meditation. The fey know this is a lifelong commitment you have made to them, to yourself, to others, and, most important of all, to the most sacred Mother Earth who sustains us all.

Faery Alert

A seguro is a very personal talisman, not to be handled by other earth-plane creatures. Some shamans report that the bottle rebels when it is passed around like a bottle of wine to be examined by those who do not or will not understand its power.

When you are not using your seguro, keep it in a safe place, preferably covered with a dark, soft cloth and out of direct light. Even when you are not using the seguro, you should commit to making thrice weekly visits to converse with it and sing together. This will strengthen the bond between you and this powerful healing object.

Faery Dream Magick

Faeries excel at dream magick. You don't need to read too many faery tales to know that strange things happen to someone who falls asleep where the faeries live.

A light jasmine tea drunk before bedtime will get you in the right mood to dream with the faeries. Decide as you drink what it is you want your dreams to reveal. A face, a prophecy, the past, the answer to a riddle, the solution to a problem, a vision of the right job for you? The list is as endless as human desire.

Although the fey will do their best to help you find what you want, sometimes they are compelled to help you find what you need. Upon waking from your dream magick, only you can decide if you've been given the directions to attain a want or a need. Some of us figure out our needs while searching for what we want. Others go after what we need and hope to find our hearts' desires along the way.

For this spell you will also need a dark blue or purple candle, preferably a tea light candle or votive you can stick deep into its holding glass. Blue and purple are colors associated with sleep, psychic power, and the upper chakras that connect us to all that is. You may choose another candle color if you wish, one you feel is more in tune with your dream magick goal.

In case you fall asleep before you can put out the flame you must be sure you will be safe. I place my candles in the sink or bathtub. If they do fall over, they go out. I'll just have some melted wax to clean up. If you have pets or children who could wander into your bedroom while the candle is burning, forgo the candle. It is not as important as the safety of your home and those it shelters.

As you drink your tea, light the candle. Say these words aloud:

> Blue as midnight, purple as dawn,
> Reveal to me what may go wrong.
> Show me my wants and show my needs,
> Tell me where I must atone for my deeds.
> In slumber deep the faeries dance,
> A face I might know I shall see perchance.
> Reveal my heart, and teach my mind,
> Let me leave this world of mine behind.
> Until a sun bright ray crosses my eye,
> Open the world of knowing this night.

Relax as you sip your tea and gaze at the candle flame. You may want to play some faery music or other dreamy, relaxing music such as native flute songs. Consider lighting incense of a scent that's pleasing to the faeries. Make sure the incense is burned out before you go to bed.

Faery Tales

Faery herbal lore recommends you keep agrimony near your bed to ward off the goblins who will be attracted by the light of your faery mind. Goblins are a type of faery who revel in upsetting humans. According to *Cunningham's Encyclopedia of Magical Herbs*, agrimony reverses negative magick that's being worked against you. It should offer extra protection during your faery dream night when you are opening yourself to foreign energies.

Focus on the precise direction you wish your dream to take. Play through several scenarios in your mind concerning your dream, but try not to limit yourself to one so that you prevent your subconscious from being open to others. When you are ready to go to sleep, make sure the incense is extinguished. Before you put out the candle, or get into bed, recite the following quatrain three times; do not speak again until you wake up in the morning.

> *Faeries dancing under a moon of blue,*
> *Show to me a dream that's true;*
> *One that guides my journey right,*
> *Blessed by day and calmed by night.*

Faery Song: The Signature Skill of the Faery Shaman

Faeries, music, song, and dance are interconnected. The songs of healing are ones faery shamans will have to learn to sing and to improvise. Faery songs for each separate occasion or need may sound somewhat alike, but they are still unique. It's the ephemeral quality underscoring the songs that makes them seem similar even when they have obvious differences in melody, time signature, and pitch.

Gary Stadler is one the few people today gifted as a channeler of faery song. The melodies on his CDs are familiar, yet they are not. Even if you're multitasking at other things, it's difficult not to stop and listen to them as they draw you deep into the world of faery. I know I've heard Stadler's music while in faeryland or in the presence of faery. Another excellent meditative CD, *Ascension to All That Is*, by Valley of the Sun, never fails to take me right into an altered state of mind.

The Enchantment of Faery Song and Dance

Many of you may already know the allure of faery song—an enchanting melody heard, but almost out of hearing range. Some of you chase the music, enraptured by its beauty. Others find your feet itching to move in ancient folk dances with the fey.

Song has long been noted in human mythology as a tool to create or destroy. Delve into any text on myth, on any culture's old pantheons, or on the history of music, and you will find song was used magickally and ritually long before it became a pleasant diversion.

Modern spiritual people create faery song in rituals, and the faery shaman should always be aware of this tool. In a ritual circle where everyone begins humming a single note, you soon hear others singing different notes that create a movement in the sound. The chords change and build for as long as the humming continues. Some of the music is mesmerizing and takes the mind straight into the otherworld.

If you are a faery shaman looking to use song on your own, start by listening to some recorded faery music. Also go out in nature and listen. If you play a musical instrument, bring it along to try and mimic the sounds of nature. Begin with a few simple notes, all within the tonic chord (the base chord of a specific musical key) of the song you feel coming to you. As you keep that one note in your working mind, let your playing mind go free to see what can be done with melodies built on that first simple chord. Be brave enough to hum the tune to your song, or to play it on your instrument.

Keep your eyes and ears open for the sounds of faery joining you. Faeries cannot resist a song, especially one written by their own shamans. Many faeries believe they bestow songwriting talent on shamans who are special to them or who have the gift of music already within themselves. Faery can also help you use song as a healing tool. Either astrally, in the silence of your room, or out in mother nature, tell the faeries what you want to do. Evoke their participation with a promise of fun.

Fey of day and fey of night,
I know you dance here in my sight;
Open my ears to sacred song,
So I may heal the weak and strong.
Create with me a melody,
One known to only me and the sidhe (pronounced shee);
One with the music to give us fun,
And filled with the power to heal one.
Let us play, dance, and sing,
Let us stand in the faery ring;
Let our hearts make music 'til the day is nigh,
And make it a song to make illness fly.

It probably won't take a lot of time for you to get into the spirit of faery music. Even people with no musical training will soon discover delightful faery music coming from their own mouths.

Folklore says that faery songs are never sung the same way twice. They are sung once, then they're either changed or discarded. My study of Irish traditional music tells me something different. Some of our most cherished folk songs are believed to be the creation of faery. Perhaps the faeries are just protecting their secrets by leaking that piece of folklore. Or, maybe they deliberately make an error each subsequent time they sing—just as Muslim rug makers intentionally weave mistakes into their carpets—to avoid the curses that can result from attempting to create perfection that can never be improved upon, even by a deity.

How It Works: The Vibration of Faery Song

Unless you are a gifted channeler, you are not going to be able to set down faery music in a tangible form. Few of us have been granted this gift. Faery tales, especially those from Celtic and Teutonic lands, give us the names of the few people who were blessed with this gift, including Turlough O'Carolan and Thomas the Rhymer.

As faery shaman you'll learn to sing with the faeries. It is not hard to follow them. The music has a contrapuntal quality, one that is easy to stray from, but still sounds good. Not only will you learn some of the favorite songs of faery, you'll learn how to initiate your own songs. And you'll learn how to go into the faery realm and entice the fey to follow a song of your own creation.

Faery Alert

If you've gotten a component of the song seriously wrong, one that would impede rather than assist your goal, you'll know it immediately—the faeries around you will stop singing. Cold silence. Start again from the beginning of the song and they'll lead you when you reach the point where the error lies, the point at which the silence began. Sometimes a faery being may step forward and correct the mistake.

You may sing to the faeries, for the faeries, or with the faeries. Each type of song weaves its own form of enchantment. For me, singing with the faeries as one of them is empowering. Singing for them makes me feel like I'm doing a poor job on a singer's audition, and I find it very uncomfortable if the fey do not join me. Yet, I can sing to the elements and the deities alone and feel a deep connection with no self-consciousness. I've never claimed to be a singer, but the fey tolerate me anyway. Don't let self-consciousness or a lack of musical talent deter you, either.

If you get really stuck for a melody, try using a standard folk song until you are accustomed to singing with the fey. It doesn't matter if it's slow or sprightly, or to which culture the melody is native, only that it resonates with you and accommodates your lyrics. If, like me, you were not blessed with a beautiful singing voice, you may have to train yourself to be comfortable singing faery song. Remember that many old folk tunes were reputed to have been gifts from the faeries to famous bards. We honor the faery by reviving their melodies.

Throughout history shamans have used song to raise the vibrational rates of their people, bringing them closer to their creator. Using faery song is developing your shaman's voice. You will soon be able to detect the difference between the sounds you are capable of producing as a faery shaman as opposed to singing along to a favorite oldie on the radio. The vibrational quality is different and you will know this without being told. Some faery shamans describe a sense of oneness with the fey, others note that their music makes a beautiful harmony or counterpoint to audible faery song. This is the same method those working with eastern traditional medicine follow when they sing the popular mantra, "Om." You are changing the atmosphere around you to create the perfect climate for healing.

Simple Lyrics That Need Your Faery Melody

The following lyrics are some I've used in magick and ritual, as well as some I was inspired to write for this book. Play around with them and see how they sound to you. Like any printed spell or ritual, the lyrics should be treated as a blueprint for creating your special faery healing songs. Do not be self-conscious about the music. Sing what you feel. Your music does not have to fit into any known rhythm signature. Many faery songs do not. Some are like extended chants, others flow, then slow, then flow again as the words inspire.

Song is an important part of the faery healing process, and also for empowering you as a faery shaman. This is the true art of soul singing, and will be your first step into more advanced faery shaman work. Once you are accustomed to singing with faeries and using their melodies for your work, you'll find you cannot wait to go back and sing with faery some more.

Here is a simple lyric announcing your pride on your new path:

> *I am on a journey to the dawn, I sing the faery shaman's song.*
> *I am on a journey in sunlight, I sing with faery, a song that is bright.*
> *I am on a journey at twilight, singing old songs by balefire light.*
> *I am on a journey beneath the moon, I sing the faery shaman's tune.*
> *Because I celebrate life I sing, I dance in and out of the faery ring.*
> *Upperworld, otherworld, dark world, and more, To the faery shaman open the door.*
> *Fly by the song that always has healed, Blessing to faery whose secrets do yield.*
> *My time is short, and their lives are long, I bless all life with faery song.*

The following lyrics are meant to be used in a drawn-out chant, longer than the ones constructed for most group rituals. Add to them as the spirit moves you.

> We are faery, we have a story,
> We must tell all, our story now.
> We all are one, under star and sun,
> The world must know this now.
> We are faery, to be heard we cry,
> So few will listen, and many will die.
> We are faery, but time is short,
> And away we fly.
> We seek to call to you, to tell a tale true,
> A tragic end we'll see, if coexist cannot we.
> We call you today, to follow us in song,
> All take heed, to save Mother Earth strong.

These lyrics are for a more rowdy chant, one that's appropriate for group rites.

> We are the fey,
> We are here today.
> We are water and fire.
> And earth and air if you desire,
> We are the fey, in spirit life is one,
> This cannot be undone,
> We are all one.
> We are one in spirit! Animals!
> We are one in spirit! Faery!
> We are one in spirit! Trees!
> We are one in spirit! Humans!
> We are one in spirit! Herbs!
> We are one in spirit! Plants!

And here's a chant that fits the standard D minor / A minor chant to which Renaissance lovers' ears are accustomed.

We are the center, of a great circle,
Within a greater circle, all within a spiral.
We are the center, of a great circle,
Within a greater circle, all within a spiral.

These lyrics should inspire a more jaunty song.

Bright faeries dance, dark faeries sing,
Some on the earth, and some on the wing.
Carefree in wellness is our world so wild,
So joyous and mirthful I feel like a child.
Dark faeries dance, bright faeries sing,
We, under the Goddess, are all one being.
Jig, and dip, and house around, ("house around" is a call used
in Irish set dancing)
Hear the earth awaken to our sound.
Sun beings sing, moon beings dance,
Inhibitions gone, we leap and we prance.
We have no other goal than to enjoy this day,
To celebrate life in the faery way.

Try this one to lure the fey to open new worlds for you to explore.

Come from rock, and cave and glen,
Tiny perfect women and tiny little men.
Today we go a hunting, like a game we play,
Our goal is simply no more than the joy of the day.
Dance with me, come and join my song,
And never, never tarry too long.
As through the heather we do roam,
Dancing and singing magick in our faeryland home.
Much to learn and much to teach,
Sometimes silent and sometimes we speak.
Open the mysteries of the healing fey,
Protect our Mother Earth for one more day.

Much work we need to do,
Much time we ask for play,
Deeper mysteries awaken,
For me and my friends, the fey.

Creating or Embellishing Your Own Lyrics: It's Easier Than You Think

Faery song does not have to rhyme to work. However, if you've practiced the Craft for a long time, and are accustomed to doing rhyming spells or rituals on the fly, you know which word endings to stay away from and which ones to go for each time so you can easily find a sensible rhyming word. End your phrases with words that have the following sounds. They are among the easiest word endings to rhyme.

- -ight: Night, sight, flight, right, kite, tight, light, might, bite, bright, trite, rite, fight, height
- -ee: Bee, be, see, she, sidhe, flee, agree, me, we, tea, sea, knee, three, ye, free, key, plea
- -eel: Feel, steal, real, meal, keel, kneel, deal, seal, reel
- -ell: Bell, fell, dell, smell, tell, well, will, knell, gel, hell, spell
- -ire: Fire, sire, tire, ire, desire, dire, mire, wire, liar, crier, shire, higher
- -all: Fall, ball, tall, call, all, gall, hall, loll, maul, pall, wall, sprawl, crawl, shawl
- -are: Dare, air, rare, stare, bare, fair, fare, hair, tear, wear, share, rare, lair, care, spare
- -ate: Slate, hate, mate, date, rate, fate, gate, gait, irate, crate, create, wait, weight, negate, state, late, bait, bate, straight, freight, debate, pate

Then there are what I call the "classic pairings" of words in earth-spirit song, chant, and ritual. These words are common to our rites and general conversations, but they have few sensible words that rhyme with them, so if you use one of these on the fly, remember you're stuck with its partner. Yes, you can buy an inexpensive, paperback rhyming dictionary, but it won't be much use to you in midsong.

- moon-soon or moon-tune
- sun-one-fun-done-ton-run
- song-gone-long-strong
- trust-must-just-lust
- roam-home-tome-loam
- Venus-penis (you expected that one, didn't you?)
- Mars-stars-bars-jars
- change-rearrange-estrange-mange-range
- blessing-guessing or blessing-assessing
- charge-large

The Faery Faker's Songbook Arsenal

If you run out of ideas for magickal songs, don't fret. Look at the healing spells in this book, or in others. Give any of them a faery, natural, earth-based twist, then put your shaman's voice to work on them.

Another way to use music, if you feel you lack talent in this area, is to adapt your words to the folk tunes you learned as a child. In elementary school most of us knew parodies to these tunes that were decidedly unflattering to our schools. They served to make us feel empowered against an authoritarian institution. They changed our perspective for an hour or a day. Change is magick, and such magick is healing.

The famous Irish bard, Turlough O'Carolan, claimed many of his melodies were gifts of the fey. He spent many nights on a faery hill or burgh and heard the music within. The famous Irish tune "Londonderry Aire," known to most of us today as "Danny Boy," was said to be a song from faery. It is popular because it is beautiful. The melody is sweet and sentimental, then rises to a crescendo, then sinks again as the tune ends.

I promise you will immediately feel the difference in a song spell when you sing it as a faery shaman. Within fifteen minutes you will probably have the essence of your own signature song, one known only to you and faery. Your signature song will identify you and help empower you when you go to faery to gather healing knowledge and energy.

9
Healing Mother Earth

Your most important work of a faery shaman is healing Mother Earth. There is a reason the planet we live on was given this title of motherhood. The natural world incubates in her soil, her womb, and bursts forth from her at the time of the harvest. Then she rests to begin the cycle again and again. In truth, our earth is a mother who never sleeps. We tell the story of Mother Earth as mythology, as science, as lessons to our children, in poetry and song. We tell it to those who wish to learn about our nature religions, and to those who simply realize that if mother dies, we die with her.

The Importance of Your New Gift

When the growing season ends in the Northern Hemisphere, it begins in the Southern. When it is daylight in the Western hemisphere, it is nighttime in the East. Subterranean tectonic plates, like large sections of a skeleton, shift and groan under thousands of pounds of pressure. Deeper inside Mother Earth, a molten core boils, waiting to erupt through a volcanic hole. As many as 2,000 electrical storms are taking place in her atmosphere at any given moment. Parts of her flood, others wait parched with drought. Some of her inhabitants starve during famine, while others enjoy her abundance.

We humans have done much to harm our mother. Now it's up to us to work with the forces of nature to heal both the damage we've wrought and that which has resulted from natural traumas.

Like all living things, Mother Earth was born to the same divine beings who created us, and, like us, she is able to die. Like all planets she has an expected lifespan. The way she is treated and the manner in which she lives will ultimately determine the length of her life. The quality of any life depends on many factors, and some are out of our control. This is where you, the new faery shaman, serve as Mother Earth's most important link between her nature spirits, her animals, and her people.

How Do We Know Mother Earth Is Alive?

We know we live on a living planet because she lets us know how she feels from time to time. We have earthquakes, rain, drought, heat waves, oxygen, blizzards, volcanos, rivers whose courses change over time. A dead planet does not have these things. Our moon, and maybe even Mars, are dead planets. They have no more bumps and grinds left to give. They make no more islands from volcanoes. They do not rewrite maps by providing killer earthquakes. They have no atmosphere or water to sustain life as we know it. Only on Mother Earth are we like children nurtured by our mother. We have a symbiotic relationship. We must care for one another and our finite resources to sustain ourselves. Like any mother, she can be made sick from abuse, neglect, poisoning, plundering, and stripping. She can become sick enough to stop being able to sustain the life she carries. And she can die. Like babes in the womb, if our mother dies, so do we.

The point of this chapter is to put shamanic fire in your belly so that you will go out and do something to help our Mother Earth. You've taken the first step by asking for and accepting initiation as a faery shaman. You are literally the one standing in between Mother Earth and her rapists. Your allies are your collected knowledge, other faery shamans, and other people who care about the environment enough to act.

A few years ago a small and very conservative church decided it would be a good idea to cut down two large oak trees estimated to be at least 150 years old. When residents asked why, the church replied it needed room for parking and expansion. The massive trunks were left to lie in the church yard for several weeks. The ten-year-old daughter of a friend, Rhiannon, was horrified by the sight as she walked home from school.

"Mommy! Look at that. Who cut down the trees? Does that hurt them? Do they feel pain? Are they crying?"

Rhiannon was amazed by her daughter's perception. No doubt on their level of existence, they were crying, and so were the fey who lived under the roots and in the branches of those trees, and the birds and squirrels who once called it home. Rhiannon told her daughter the trees were hurting, they were crying, and they were actually now in the process of dying.

"What can we do? Can they be put back together?" the daughter asked.

"No, they are dying and can't be fixed now," responded Rhiannon, who used this moment to teach her daughter about the feelings of other people and things, and how some actions cannot be undone, no matter how much we want them to be.

A Faery Shaman's Work with Mother Nature

After you do all the practical things you can think of, it is time to allow your faery partners to tell you what you need to do next. You can make this connection by returning to faeryland through the same gates of fire you entered for your initiation. If you have a wild place in nature in mind—especially if it is an area being marked for destruction—go there and watch for the natural spirits to appear and speak to you. Identify yourself as a faery shaman who has come to help.

If this is your first time going into nature as a faery shaman, the fey may be hesitant or distrustful at first. Though they know by the energy of your talisman that their Kings and Queens have put their stamp of approval on you, the faery have been fooled before. Be gentle with the spirits who appear to you and let them lead the conversation. In fact, this is good advice to take in encounters with any spirit beings you meet. You'll get much more useful information if you listen rather than talk.

How to Relocate a Plant

Something you might be asked to do, but which you cannot predict, is to relocate a plant. In fact, the plant itself might ask you to move it and its soul to a safer location. This shows either great trust or great fear on the part of the nature spirit. It may be one of the last of its kind. It might be one that will someday provide us a cure for disease, or be cultivated as a food, or any of millions of possibilities. We have already hacked thousands of plant species to extinction and we may never know what miracles they could have offered us if we had only stopped to listen.

If you're not a green thumb, which I admit I am not, find a book or a friend or neighbor who always seems able to keep beautiful things blooming all year long. Ask for this person's advice on a plant you wish to move. If someone asks why you are interested in saving one small plant that you cannot even name, just say that you are new to the study of botany, and this plant appears so unique that you cannot let it die until you know more about it. That should stop the questions. Gardeners understand.

When you return to the plant, ask it again if it is sure it wants you to move it. You will also need to ask where it wants to go. It may be that the current environment is too wet or too dry, or it may just not feel safe and request sanctuary at your home. Talk this over in detail with the plant faery. It may be a danger to your children and pets, or the soil at your home may be just as dry or soaked as the place the plant is in now. You may not have a yard, but a terrarium or window box. Make sure this is a satisfactory arrangement with the spirit of the plant before doing anything.

This is just one of many scenarios you may come across. Other plants you encounter may have other needs or requests. Some might need more water, others may need more sun. Do what you can for each plant, within the boundaries of your personal ethics and abilities.

How to Encourage Cross Pollination

In April 2007 I was honored to be a guest at the Oklahoma Pagan Alliance's Beltane Festival. One of the Alliance members is a beekeeper who gave a detailed, though somewhat grim, presentation about the endangerment of our cross pollinators. This not only includes bees, which are her specialty, but also birds, hummingbirds, and butterflies. Butterflies; now that really made me stop and think for a moment. Only a week earlier my mother had mentioned something about not seeing as many butterflies these days as we used to see. Or fireflies either. We both remembered when they were so copious, we had a yard full of them even around our inner-city home when I was a child.

At the festival I learned about viruses that have invaded beehives all over the world, and the desperate efforts scientists and environmentalists are using to combat the problem. I also learned that Albert Einstein predicted humanity would have less than four years to live if our cross pollinators were to become extinct. Modern zoologists estimate we would have less than half that time due to the selling of hybrid food, plants, or seeds rendered sterile before being sold, to keep farmers coming back to buy more each planting season. As we continue to destroy our forests, gardens, and prairies, it follows that we also lose the cross pollinators who feed from, or make other food from, this plant life. Cross pollination is necessary for species to thrive and evolve. Inbreeding causes problems that become apparent after several generations, whereas cross pollination provides genetic diversity in plants, making species stronger and able to produce greater yields.

Saving our cross pollinators is an easier task than saving endangered plant species. If you want to help ensure the survival of cross pollinators, here are some things you can do:

- If you have land a beekeeper can use, please find one and let him or her know you welcome a hive on your property. This way you are providing a place for the bees in a new area to pollinate, and the beekeeper does all the work.
- Look for flowers in your landscaping plans that attract the birds and bees. Certain colors and scents are more enticing than others, and these can change throughout their feeding season.
- Put up and maintain hummingbird feeders.

- Put up and maintain bird feeders and houses. Winter birds will rely on you as a food supply year round.
- Buy your honey from local beekeepers. Popular folklore even says this is the healthiest way to go and can help you resist allergies to local pollens.
- Plant berry bushes or shrubs that attract birds. Birds will fly up to five miles to feed on berries. The seeds they drop will result in new bushes for birds farther away to eat and spread the seeds. (Please be aware of which ones are toxic if you have children or pets using this area too.) Blackberries and blueberries are most attractive to cross pollinators.
- Orange and apple trees are most attractive to honeybees.
- Honeysuckle is the most attractive vine plant to faeries, and bees seem to like it too.
- Cross pollinators have been used successfully in the pollination of hothouse tomatoes and other fruits grown in a controlled environment.
- Experiment with outdoor decor and foliage that attract butterflies or hummingbirds.
- Take insects and bugs from your home and place them outdoors. This is another food source for birds.
- Consider planting flowering trees. Not only are they pretty, they also attract birds and bees. Your choices will depend on the climate in which you live but cherry trees, orange trees, magnolias, dogwoods, and apple trees are good choices. Most of these grow quickly and maintain themselves at a height that will not interfere with your neighbor's landscaping, nor do they grow tall enough to interfere with utility wires.

Ongoing experimentation with biotic pollination, the term used for cross pollination carried out by the animal kingdom, is also addressing this problem. Entomophily is the scientific umbrella term for pollination requiring the help of insects, beetles, moths, and flies. Zoophily covers pollination assisted by vertebrates such as birds, bats, hummingbirds, sunbirds, and fruit flies. Wind and water carry cross pollination, too, with varying degrees of success.

"It has always been customary to leave offerings for the faeries. Milk and cream, and sometimes honey were traditional offerings in Wales, Ireland, and England . . . Be sure to maintain your part of the relationship you wish to have with the Faery Realm by making offerings . . . Allow yourself to be part of the reciprocal cycle of the energies for each season."—Margie McArthur, *Faery Healing: The Lore and the Legacy*

Faery lore tells us that small faeries often ride on the backs of birds, bees, butterflies, and other small flying animals. Leave libations outdoors for the faeries, and they may ride in on their flying friends and discover your cross-pollination paradise. Though this is a vast subject for another book, our cross pollinators are in danger of extinction, with frightening repercussions we can only imagine, such as famine.

Conservation and Recycling

We are now hearing the first screams of panic as our climate changes and the natural resources we've always depended on diminish. Faeries of snow, elementals of earth and rain, and plant spirits can tell you what they need locally to remain alive. Listen and do what you can for them.

Here's a list of simple things you can do to help slow down or reverse the destruction and depletion of Mother Earth. Pick one or two and follow through on your plan. If every household just did one extra thing each day to assist the environment, it would buy us a year of time for each day we succeed at our task. These should already be familiar to you since they have been in print and on the television daily for at least the past five years.

- Separate trash into compost, burnable, plastic recyclable, glass recyclable, aluminum recyclable, paper recyclable, and mechanical recyclable.
- Make sure each division of your trash is disposed of at a recycling center where it will be used to make future products.
- Some charities depend on donations of recyclable products, particularly aluminum, to help them meet their financial goals. If

you are part of a club, coven, or any other small group, take the lead in organizing members to collect aluminum cans and donate them to a local charity.

- Drive a smaller vehicle and save gas. Carpool whenever possible.
- Replace incandescent light bulbs with long-lasting compact fluorescent ones.
- Use public transportation whenever possible, or select one day a week to take the bus or train instead of driving your car. Organize your coworkers to commit to a one-day-a-week "no driving" pact.
- Mow your lawn less often. Avoid using poisonous chemicals that harm insects, birds, and wildlife and seep into ground water.
- Consider whether a rich green lawn in the heat of summer is really more important than conserving the water supply. Perhaps you can replace lush grass with hardier wild ones or drought-resistant plants.
- Cut back on the amount of water you use when showering or bathing.
- Don't let water run when brushing your teeth.
- Adopt a highway or lakeshore and pick up litter regularly.
- Wear warm clothes in winter and turn down the heat at home and in your workplace. In summer, do the reverse and use air conditioning sparingly.
- Refuel cars, lawnmowers, and other petroleum-powered vehicles after sunset when heat does not evaporate the gasoline fumes into the atmosphere.
- Do not bundle up dried autumn leaves, put them in plastic bags, and let someone take them to a landfill. Leaves are among the most biodegradable substances we have. Mow them into a mulch, compost them, or just leave them to mow in the spring. Leaves help protect the roots of the trees, and when mowed in spring, they feed the grass. Some communities will take lawn clippings and autumn leaves in paper bags if the paper is made of a special biodegradable material.

- The same goes for animal waste. Don't put doggie doo-doo in a plastic bag where it will remain enshrined forever in a landfill. Take it indoors and flush it down the toilet.
- Keep animal waste far from places where faeries dwell unless you are landscaping with high quality fertilizers and have let the faeries know what you are doing and why. Listen for their input. They can tell you the best time and method for fertilizing an area. Some vineyards have staff or owners who claim that by listening to the spirits of the land they achieved a dramatic increase in yield. A book called *The Elves of Lily Hill Farm* (Llewellyn, 1997), by Penny Kelly, is a detailed look at how this type of partnership works. Penny and her husband decided to buy a vineyard on which to make their living. Penny made mistakes which would harm rather than help their efforts. Most of her care of the grapevines was obtained from by-the-book advice. Once a trio of elven fey appeared to her to give counsel—and she decided to listen to them—the vineyard's yield exceeded all expectations.
- If you work in a place that does not recycle, volunteer to monitor this task, or offer to head a committee with other concerned employees. You just might find more faery shamans than you thought you would.
- Join an Adopt-a-Median group, one that volunteers to keep a section of a street or highway clean of debris. In Indiana, many of these areas are part of a wildflower project, a place to allow the native wildflowers of the state to thrive in their natural habitat. Remember that each flower contains a faery soul.

Spells and Rituals to Heal Mother Earth

Practical spell casting is another part of the faery shaman's work. Folk magick is natural magick, just like natural healing. These time-honored practices have been passed down in oral tradition for generations, by families who lived and worked on the land. You do not have to espouse any particular religion to do any of these spells and rituals. There is nothing sacrilegious about using magick to heal Mother Earth.

Prerequisites for Faery Magick

There are four standard prerequisites for faery magick. Follow this simple formula when performing spells.

- Need: A need arises—a real need, not just something you want.
- Desire: This creates a desire, which can grow very fierce. It becomes the energy that drives the magick and links you to faery.
- Knowledge: You must have knowledge to make your magick work; here's where the faeries can help you.
- Silence: Keep silent about your efforts. Talking about it gives away its power and allows other people to accumulate energies that can counteract your own.

Three Ethical Tests

These three ethical tests come from Eastern and Pagan traditions. The law of not doing to others what you would not want done to you, however, is found in every society and spiritual sect in the world.

- So long as your efforts harm no one, then proceed as you will.
- You alone must accept responsibility for the outcome of any actions or decrees you make.
- All you do comes back to you, sometimes in multiples.

If these criteria fit your efforts, then forge ahead knowing that you're going to be helping someone in need. Your goodwill shall spread and create more goodwill among the beings on our planet.

Planetary Healing Spells and Rituals

Thanks to Earth Day and a newly awakened human consciousness about the illnesses of Mother Earth, more people than ever are aware that we are putting the earth in danger. People from all walks of life, all economic and social backgrounds, and from all faiths are more aware of the packaging they buy and how this trash is disposed of after use. Prayers, chants, and actions—such as recycling—are being enacted every day by diverse people with one goal in mind. Healing Mother Earth for future generations to enjoy. Mother Earth is more than an ornament, or a large waste receptacle, she is and must continue to be our basic life support system.

A Simple Earth Healing Ritual

How many times have you heard or read the phrase, "Think Globally, Act Locally"? The world is a huge place when looked upon by one person, but all together we are more than seven billion people looking out the window and thinking what we can do to make things better.

The best thing for you to do, either alone or with a group of friends, is to adopt a section of undeveloped land and promise to be its guardian. You need only yourselves and a small gift for each of the elemental rulers. Announce to the faeries in this locale that you are committing yourself to keeping this tract of land clean and habitable. If your help is not wanted you will know it. You or someone with you will say, "This place feels creepy, let's get outta here." More often you will feel a welcoming presence, one that produces a sense of mission and calmness on everyone.

Select someone to invite the ruler of each of the four cardinal directions. As this is done, the gift you brought for that ruler should be laid in the corresponding quarter.

Because your goal is to make the land clean and attractive, you should choose gifts such as bird seed, squirrel corn, or small animal food, to feed the animals of the area. Keep these things on the ground. Items made of glass, stone, or metal will only make the area appear cluttered, and it could pose a danger to those who come to the area because they are drawn to its tranquility.

If you have a small group, you should space yourselves evenly around the area. Ideally, you can gather enough concerned people to stand holding hands around the entire adopted tract. If you cannot reach one another, ask the faeries and other nature spirits in the area to fill in the gaps.

Have everyone visualize the nature spirits joining you, hand in hand, around the adopted land.

You may choose any course of action that pleases you. Chant, sing, make affirmations (which will come out as chants), or whatever else you feel moved to do. While this is taking place, visualize the entire world being within your encircled area and pour healing energy into it. Ask permission of the fey to draw energy from them to help you.

Also, please don't be afraid to start a chant fearing you will be thought silly or crazy. Your intent is more important than your words.

Consider these:

- Land of life support just beneath our feet, help us to help you when here we shall meet.
- Blessing to Mother Earth we send, so life and beauty shall never end.
- Mother Earth, home to us all, we pledge you our respect, one and all.
- Circling Mother Earth we see, that our current path must not be.
- Earth Mother, Earth Mother, crying out in need, here we are to do the deed.
- We are a circle within a larger one, promising Mother Earth her life shall be won.

Silliness and profound thoughts should go into any chant, which, by the way, does not have to rhyme to be effective. It just makes it easier to remember the words. Go with the words the fey put into your head and have fun while injecting some serious healing into your adopted tract of land. Be sure to follow it up with weekly visits to do the routine cleaning chores.

A Simple Spell to Care for Mother Earth

Spells are a formalized method for sending your will out into the universe so it can return with what you asked to have. In this case you want to take care of our ailing Mother Earth.

For this spell you will need a globe of any size, a glass of water in which rosemary has been all night, your own breath, and lots of visualization.

You may do this spell anywhere that the water will not ruin flooring or furniture. Once you have selected that spot, take your globe and water glass to it and settle in so you are comfortable.

Hold the globe in your hands. Spin it, touch it, pour healing healing energy into it with the help of nearby faeries you may request to assist you. Allow your thoughts to be of a perfect world, healthy and whole.

Caress the earth the way a mother would caress your face if you were sick. Project your visualization of what you want into the globe which is now representing the entire planet. Create a simple spell using the desires you have. It can sound something like this:

> *Here we are, both human and fey,*
> *We will a change day by day;*
> *Mother Earth we want you well,*
> *Or life will become hell,*
> *Healed, cleaned, and war-free be,*
> *As we will it, so must it be.*

You can also do this spell with others and each person can take the globe and make a statement of desire for the near future. Go around the circle until every participant has had a chance to hold the globe and make an affirmation. Again, do not forget that the simplest spells are often the most effective. No one has long paragraphs of lines to remember, and everyone can relax and put their full willpower reserves where it is needed most.

10

Healing Your Emotions with Faery Assistance

Faeries are emotion, wrapped up in a pretty package. For centuries people who sought and found faeries reported how easily their feelings were hurt, and how quick they were to rejoice over some small token of kindness or honor. Though some people claim to have seen faery tears, in general, faeries don't deal with many negative feelings and do not indulge—perhaps cannot sustain—long bouts of depression. That's a recipe for a stress-free existence.

The Connection Between Faeries and Human Emotions

No one has to remind us that the stresses of our fast-paced human lives impact our emotional and physical health. This is an area in which faery can help us greatly. Though they possess emotions, and can become violently outraged at certain behaviors, their emotional upheavals are brief. In general, most of the fey are cheerful and playful, even when they are working. They can help us deal with emotional blows, protect those of us who are empaths, and teach us the joys of faery song and dance.

The faery realm is the place to turn to when you need to ramp up your mood fast. The trick to making this work for you rather than against you is to appear cheerful as you enter their realm. Left to their own devices, the fey will feel it polite to mimic your state of mind. Whether you are sitting alone in nature, or you have traveled to faeryland in your astral body, force yourself to appear and behave cheerfully, regardless of how you truly feel. The faery love to play, and if you tell them that is the reason you are joining them, they will welcome you. Soon their buoyant emotions will boost yours, too.

The vast majority of faeries of the nature spirit variety are ready and willing to assist you in healing. The nature spirits are a caste of faery that doesn't usually experience too many emotional roller coaster rides. These faeries concern themselves with healing and nurturing. If a faery shaman can pick up on those qualities, then he or she will advance through the world of faery with greater ease and learn healing faster because of this immense well of compassion. After you become a faery shaman they will redouble their efforts for you because you are creating an exchange of energy you both can use. Constantly drawing energy from faery and never giving any back in return, however, is a quick way to find yourself on the receiving end of their anger.

With the fey you can play games, dance, sing, eat, and drink—just remember to keep an eye on the time! If you went into the faery realm feeling bad, and now are emotionally drunk and feeling no pain, you could become entrapped in the world of faery, or pine away for their world once you leave.

Faery and humans inhabit two different realms for a reason. We are not the same species no matter how many places our interests meet. Neither can survive without the other, but neither can we survive living in the other's realm. Faery would die if held captive in our world, and we would die if we remained in theirs. Faeries do not always understand the motives for human emotions any more than we understand what upsets or angers them.

The Problems of the Empath or Clairsentient

An empath is a person whose psychic energy centers, or chakras, take on the emotions of those around them. Those emotions then manifest in the empath. The stronger the feelings are, the more impact they have on the empath. Sometimes there is enough disturbance that the empath's life is curtailed. People involved in nature spirituality are often natural empaths, or else they become empathic from years of opening themselves to the energies around them.

A clairsentient is someone who is impacted by the emotions of spirits and other denizens of unseen worlds, which can be every bit as jarring as confronting the emotions of living humans.

Long before I had a wise teacher who could put a name to my problem, I was aware that I could be reduced to melancholy and tears by people or places that didn't affect anyone else. When I was eighteen I went with a group from my college to Appomattox Court House, Virginia, where the American Civil War came to an end. As our vehicle turned off the highway and onto the small country road that ran between large fields surrounded by wooden fencing, I was struggling to fight back tears.

By the time we pulled into the welcome center, I was sobbing like a baby. I felt very foolish. Fortunately my friends blew my emotions off, thinking my reaction was due to the fact that I was the great-granddaughter of a man who was in the 27th Virginia Cavalry. After sitting through a movie about the surrender of the Confederacy's General Robert E. Lee to the Union's General Ulysses S. Grant, I felt fine again. Then we all went out to explore the old area of the town where the buildings had been preserved just as they were on that April day in 1865. With the help of my friends I was able to get through the rest of the excursion and enjoy it. What I could not do was be in the house where the actual surrender took place. In fact, it was difficult for me to even stand too close to it. There was more than enough emotional static in the atmosphere to knock any empath on the ground.

It was in front of this house where Lee's troops stood waiting for their leader. Most of them did not expect to be told to go home, the war was over. Many grown men burst into tears vowing to follow their beloved General if he wished to go on fighting. Lee himself was in turmoil, and rode off quickly toward his own home in Arlington, on a hill overlooking the Potomac River and the city we now call Washington, D.C. His family had been removed from the home and its surrounding land was in the process of becoming a cemetery for dead soldiers. Today we call Lee's land The Arlington National Cemetery.

Had I known about nature spirits and their deep emotions, emotions that had lived and died with the trees and plants around me, I would have reached out to them to take away some of that intense sorrow and ground it back into the earth.

My first real teacher in natural spirituality identified me as an empath, and possible clairsentient, and began to show me ways to block unwanted emotional energies. Even the most cheerful person cannot remain in a state of invigoration forever. We all have our moments of sadness, reflection, and regrets.

Empaths who feel and are jolted by emotions outside of themselves are often the ones who most easily connect with faery, however. The capricious world of faery is very emotional. In fact, their world is as given to bouts of emotional storms as ours is to thunderstorms.

Healing as a Self-Discipline

It takes more than willpower and knowledge to heal. It also takes common sense, compassion, endless study, and the ability to set the ego aside once in a while to let someone with more experience take over a healing problem. The wisest healers know when to ask for help.

Begin a daily ritual of holding an image in your head. Do not get frustrated when your mind wanders. This happens to the most gifted of seekers. Once you can maintain images for a period of at least fifteen minutes, add an affirmation to the image in your mind. Make it positive and, when possible, try to make your words in the present tense, not the future tense. Putting magick into "tomorrow" will only keep your goals forever one day away.

Practice drawing energy up from Mother Earth, the powers above, and the faeries. When you are full of this energy, mentally shape it into what you want it to become. Send this out into the universe with or without spoken words. What is put out there always returns to the sender, so give it your best.

This sounds very simple, but in practice it is not. The conscious mind gets bored and wants to go where it wants to go, not where you direct it. Without a chant or song in your head to help hold it, you will have more wandering than you would like. Just remember that every shaman was once a beginner. You are lucky. You have the fey to help you keep your mind where it belongs. One day you'll sit down to practice this and discover you have little or no trouble making it work.

Be sure to reward your faery helpers with an appropriate gift when this occurs.

Your knowledge will keep expanding, and someday you will have your chance to step in and help a new faery shaman initiate perform a full healing ritual. I hope that experience is both thrilling and humbling for you.

Spells to Heal Your Emotions

Some humans treat their emotional issues with drugs, alcohol, or other harmful substances that were never intended to be used as permanent fixes. Follow faery rules and you will have a better alternative, a secret place to go whenever you need an emotional lift. The realm of faery is always waiting for you and will always heal your mental state, enabling you to go out and face the mundane world again.

Faery Love Spell

Faery love spells are legendary for making even the most nondescript person appear to be the most attractive man or woman on the face of the earth. These legends arose because the fey themselves, who are often the objects of human desire, are incredibly beautiful.

Most faery love spells have a manipulative element about them. Pagans and Witches try to adhere to the Pagan Rede of "Harm None," which says it is wrong to infringe on the free will of another being. In the "Faery Come Hither Spell," which appears later in this chapter, we will unleash the manipulative nature of the fey for those brave enough to risk the threefold bounce back.

This spell, though, is more subtle. You'll need fresh orange blossoms, or apple blossoms if you must. (As a last resort order them from a florist.) You will also need a small bit of true orange blossom essential oil. The scent is sweet without being cloying, and has been associated with marriages for a long time. My grandmother's wedding ring was etched with a circle of orange blossoms when she married in 1921.

Mentally picture the love of your life being attracted to you, as you weave the flowers into a chaplet (a small crown for your head). Men can do this too. The custom in most nature spiritualities says it is just as appropriate for a man to wear a chaplet as it is for a woman, especially in traditions that honor faery.

Dip your fingers in the orange blossom oil and dot it around the chaplet. (If the oil runs and becomes absorbed by the chaplet, you are using too much oil. Rub in what you already have, then proceed with smaller amounts.) You might also want to scent a ribbon and tie it to the back of the chaplet, so that it trails down your back. The easiest way to scent satin is to hold it in the smoke of orange blossom incense. (Use plain orange incense if orange blossom is not available.) Another option is to soak the ribbon overnight in orange peel shavings. The next day, rinse the ribbon under clear, cool water and let it dry. It should retain its scent for about a week.

Faery Alert

Keep your magick spells to yourself. Being silent about your magickal work prevents interference from others. Even a person who doesn't believe in magick and thinks you are crazy can generate negative energies—or petty jealousies—that may disrupt your spells.

Dance around your home and sing a song to call your as-yet unknown lover to you, while wearing the chaplet. Delight in the scent of the orange blossoms. Chant the following incantation, or one of your own creation. It can help you get started, but remember it's a blueprint only. It gives you the pieces, but you should substitute and alter the spell until it feels right for your situation.

> Orange blossoms scenting the worlds all around,
> Lover of mine hear this faery song sound;
> From deep within the world of fey,
> To the present search I make this day.
> With faery help below and from above,
> I cast my net to my soul mate, my love;
> When s/he hears my lonely siren song,
> By my side s/he'll come 'ere long.

Repeat this spell several times a week until it manifests.

Healing a Broken Heart Spell

This spell is intended to heal your broken heart after a loss or disappointment. You want to radiate happiness and self-confidence, and become aware of things you didn't even realize brought you happiness until you began this spell.

You will need a number of small, polished gemstones for this spell. A handful should be enough. Metaphysical stores and online resources have plenty of these for sale, or you can tumble your own stones in a lapidary. You'll also need a piece of cardboard about five inches tall by five inches wide. You may paint the cardboard any color that makes you feel joyous, attractive, and successful—deserving of love and a happy future. Use more than one color if you like. Toss some glitter into the paint if you feel festive.

Cut the cardboard in two pieces. On one piece of cardboard draw half a heart, so that the center is flush against the edge of the cardboard—it will make a whole heart when joined with the other half. Begin gluing the stones to the cardboard.

As you work, take time to focus on the goal of your spell. As you place each stone on the cardboard heart, say something like:

> *A green stone for new beginnings;*
> *Rose quartz for romance and inner peace;*
> *A quartz crystal for drawing away negative thoughts;*
> *A tiger's eye for prosperity;*
> *Carnelian for attraction.*

It doesn't matter what stones you use or how and where you place them in the heart. It is more important to enchant them with your energy and your need to be healed.

Repeat the process on the other piece of cardboard. Then tie the two halves together with a ribbon to make a whole heart again, and chant:

> *Heart of gold,*
> *Never grows old.*
> *Heart of day,*
> *Shines my way.*

Heart of moon,
Hears my tune.
Heart of mine,
Feels so fine.
The love I need,
I receive.
The broken pain,
Is on the wane.
I feel strong,
I am not wrong.
The best I deserve,
For me I reserve.
By faeries' delight,
My will comes to light.
Love of my dreams,
Come forth and be seen.

Put the heart under your mattress or in the bottom of a dresser drawer for at least one lunar month. During this time do positive things to get over the old relationship. Go out with friends, paint a room of your house, get a new haircut, take a class, take up a sport, join a gym, etc. Do anything to get yourself into a new social routine.

One day you will realize you have not thought of your ex all day long. This is the day to remove the cardboard heart, untie it, and scatter all the beautiful stones over a faery shrine. This is your "thank you" offering for the fey's assistance in helping you find your new life.

Faery "Come Hither" Perfume

Seduction is one of the first characteristics we think of when we start to dwell on the wonders of the world of faery: exotic scents carried on the wind to a distant lover, followed by the faint strains of a compelling melody that draws in its quarry.

To prepare for this spell, go into the world of faery. Ask to be taken to the place where love spells grow. You will be taken to a place where plants that induce feelings of romance grow. It will most likely be a world of lush springtime, where a warm sun shines and spring colors are everywhere. Small winged faeries fly among the foliage, laughing and tempting. A hint of eroticism is in the atmosphere here. One look and one sniff will tell you why it is called a place where "love spells grow."

Announce that you are a faery shaman who has considered all other options and consequences, but you have decided you want a Come Hither Perfume and Song. Allow the fey to question you. They, too, know the consequences of interfering in free will, but they are your partners, not your mommies, and they will not stop you from doing this if it's what you really want.

Begin to wander through the flowers and wild growth, hunting for a scent that you find alluring. Once you find one, see if its nature spirit will talk to you about its properties. This will help you get a better idea of whether you want to use it or not. Depending upon your style of perfume, you might prefer single note scents or blends. You might also prefer light florals to heavier herbals. Men usually like to wear woodsy scents, musks, and blends with citrus bases. Keep the person you are trying to attract in mind as you choose scents. This will help you narrow down your selection.

Once you have your list of scents to start blending, thank the fey and leave faeryland to go shopping for the oils and essences you have chosen. Some oils are very expensive, and this may cause you to rethink your spell. Do not use synthetic oils. They do not smell the same on the skin as they do in the bottle, and if they are dried or burned they can turn into horrible smells. Nothing "Come Hither" about it at all.

Use a neutral oil—almond, safflower, or olive—as a base. It is best to mix oils in a dark glass eye dropper bottle you can purchase from a pharmacy. Make sure you buy two lids, one to cap off the oil blend when not in use, and another that includes the rubber stopper. The rubber will decay quickly in oils, so you want to save your droppers for applying the oil.

Once you've mixed your oils into the base, set the bottle in a dark place so the scents can fuse, or "marry" as some herbalists prefer to say. Seven days is the usual amount of time to accomplish this task. Each day turn the bottle a few times to keep the scents mixing, but do not bruise the delicate oils by shaking them. Also, keep records of exactly how many drops of which oil you are using. Don't think you will remember. If you find a wonderful scent that makes a strong spell, you will be devastated if you can't recreate it.

After seven days, open the bottle and inhale the scent you have created. Is it everything you expected it to be? Is something missing? Is it too floral? Could it use some musk or some heady herbs? Is it too heavy? Could it use some lighter notes?

If you're not 100 percent happy with the potion, return with the bottle to faeryland, going back to the place where you gathered your ingredients in the first place. Ask for help in fine-tuning the scent. A nature spirit—probably more than one—may come forward and offer you a sniff of what he or she has to share. Don't take more than one scent at a time. You don't want to kill your perfume under a too-cloying scent.

I also recommend that when you add the new oil, add it only to half of your perfume mixture. Use only one or two drops, then examine the scent the next day to see if it smells the way you want it to. If not, place one or two drops of another scent in the other half of the mixture. By the next day you should be getting an idea of how these will marry.

As you can tell, this is not a quick spell to prepare. You'll have lots of time to reconsider the advisability of manipulating someone else's free will. You can still bail out at this point and direct your Come Hither spell toward "someone right for you who is also seeking his or her true love" rather than aiming at only one target.

If you have used any oils that are caustic or could cause irritation if applied to the skin, put a small amount of the oil on a bra or pair of panties, where it will not contact your skin. Oils have very strong odors and you will only need a small amount to give you that "floating in a cloud of seductive scent" effect.

Wearing the scent should help you keep your goal in mind. So much of successful magick is based upon triggering the mind to seek your goal once your ritual preparation starts. Without that subconscious kickoff, your spell will be much less effective.

If you change your mind and decide you prefer someone else, dispose of the "Come Hither" perfume blend or alter it. Otherwise, it will continue making you think about a lover you do not want.]

Go into the faery realm, back to the place where you obtained the scents. Solicit opinions concerning the smell and the strength of the energy you have put into the perfume while making it. You may be surprised to find you concocted a spell bottle for what you need most, not what you think you want most.

Close your eyes and relax. As you begin to rock and sway under the spell of the fey, listen to their heart song around and within you. Notice your own heart beating in rhythm to their music. They are giving you a valuable key to your spell. Faery song is almost irresistible to human ears, and if faery is willing to teach you one of its secret songs to attract the lover of your choice, be smart and grateful enough to learn it word for word, note for note.

You will soon find that you and the faeries are singing the same melody. Some may break off into harmonies that enhance the beauty of the song for you. Capture in your memory the emotion and spirit of the moment. You will have to sing this song as you don the perfume, and perhaps hum it while in the presence of your lover-to-be.

I've never seen this spell fail, but I have seen it draw the wrong people together. Think carefully about what you really want. You might just get it and wish you had not.

Erasing Someone from Your Mind

We know from fairy tales that the enchantment of forgetting is also a power of the faery. They can make us lose track of time, dim the memory of pain, and restore a sense of happiness we thought we'd lost. This is part of the charm of faery. The more we need, the more faery will try to provide.

Each night before you go to sleep, light a black candle and spend some time gazing at it. Black is a color that absorbs all light; it also absorbs unwanted energies, such as the memory of someone you need to forget. At least this spell will help you stop thinking constantly about the person.

Next, take a garland of forget-me-nots or a simple clover chain and break it into small pieces as you gaze at the candle. Imagine all unwanted memories flowing from your head into the candle. As you watch the flame, recite the following:

> *Erase my mind, wipe clean my mental slate,*
> *I ask this with no malice, I created my fate.*
> *Now I ask that the memories be gone,*
> *I made a mistake and I judged (him or her) wrong.*
> *Erase my mind, wipe clean my mental slate,*
> *I ask this with no malice, I do not hate.*
> *I want only to forget, the time so bad for me,*
> *Faery beings, please help me, so mote it be.*

Then extinguish the candle. Repeat this spell each night until the candle has completely burned down.

Faery-Borne Illnesses

The nature of the faery realm is emotional, and many "illnesses" can be contracted from them, which will throw off your emotional balance if you are not careful to establish good barriers between their emotions and your own. If you find that you do not feel better after spending time in faeryland, or if your emotional slump turns into physical illness, you may have caught a faery illness, one that was never meant to find its way into the body of a human being.

Because we live in different worlds, we have different immunities, and a virus to which faery is immune could make a human very sick. Faeries of the nature spirit variety do not intentionally pass along illness to their shamans or to those who love them. Remember, as a faery shaman, you are partners with these beings. They do not want to harm you.

A bizarre paradox, it's emotional illness that faery is most likely to pass on to you, even though emotional problems are also the ones they can most readily help you heal.

The melancholy often associated with pining away for the bright world of faery was called being "elf shot" in medieval times. Small arrow-shaped stones were occasionally found in areas that were once populated by races of humans, now long extinct. Archaeological findings attributed them to the faeries.

Other illnesses were caused by "Ill Winds." These were the faeries of what we now call the Unseelie Court. The term originated in Scotland and referred to a band of windblown faeries with negative energy and harmful intent. Various types of seizures, Sudden Infant Death Syndrome, and strokes were blamed on the Ill Winds.

Modern spiritual seekers know all too well the feeling of astral parasites, beings from otherworlds who cannot gather their own energy and must suck it out of unaware travelers they find in their world. The faeries who become your allies through the shamanic initiation are as good as having your own army. They will come when called, just as your spirit guides or deities do when asked (never commanded). They will help you detach these beings from yourself so you do not bring them into your earth plane world to continue feasting.

Trading Places: How We Can Heal Faery Emotions

Occasionally faeries get sick. Throughout folklore there are numerous accounts of talented people—usually herbalists, shamans, or followers of nature spiritualities—who were summoned to help cure a faery illness.

Midwifery is often recounted as a way in which humans assist faeries. Perhaps faery's longevity makes births rare and difficult, nature's way of population control. Sometimes faeries become sick from poisons introduced by humans into their natural homes.

As an initiated faery shaman, you will be counted upon to come and offer healing whenever the need arises. In many ways you will be to faery what hospitals and doctors are to humans. You will need to be discerning if voices or spirits appear to you at night—listen carefully before you say that you are too tired to talk, so please go away.

Healing sick faeries—even colonies of them who seem to be in the midst of an epidemic—is not difficult for a faery shaman. We use the same energy tools we employ in other aspects of our magick and ritual practices to direct energy to the sick faeries.

The easiest method is to draw healing energy up into your own body from Mother Earth. Allow it to fill you until you feel your fingers begin to tingle, then discharge the energy into the faery or colony who needs your help. You might have to repeat this process as many as five times. Every culture has its sacred or lucky numbers, and the fey seem to respond to five, though sometimes three attempts may be enough, and other times you'll need more.

If you are faced with an entire colony of sick nature spirits, your culprit probably is not a virus, but a manmade catastrophe yet unknown to the human population. Forest land destruction, dangerous fertilizer, poison weed killer, etc. How would you feel if these things were going to be done in your neighborhood with no concern for your safety and no forewarning to the inhabitants to find someplace safer until the "event" is over?

When you encounter cries for help from a large faery community, the fey may not have the words to describe the fear, much less the ability to provide a solution. You will need to track down the source of the epidemic. Chemical pollution by humans or human workplaces are the most frequent offenders. Assure them that you will take action on their behalf. You may not be able to stop the cause of their distress, but you can offer forewarning and assistance in relocating. Faeries are very sentimental and many may choose to remain in their natural homes and either die or be pulled into the astral world forever.

If you can get the press or an environmental group interested in the situation, you will buy time for the faery to relocate. A court could prevent further destruction, pollution, or development. It sometimes takes years for chemical pollution to establish a pattern of devastation in the human population, but faery is more sensitive and will succumb to ill effects more quickly.

With the mind goes the body, and emotions are all over the place in faery. Nature spirits are capricious, sensitive, and they expect immediate help from their shaman partners when they or their world is in crisis. In talking with the fey it is possible to come up with solutions to problems they would never have considered on their own. This is no different than how we are in their world. There are unintentional secrets in both worlds, and resolutions to problems or health crises may be easier than either of us thinks while mired down in our own misery from which it seems there is no way out.

Faery Healing Spell #1: Soothing Chaotic Emotions

Anyone who has the slightest understanding of mob psychology understands how easy it is for a small grievance to become a call to revolution. Those who feel wronged, with no clear path to solving a problem, can whip a crowd of thousands into a dangerous mob in a matter of minutes. There is no sense of goal or order behind these escalating feelings, and very little chance that the course of action chosen in a swelling atmosphere of injustice will be successful. An angry mob almost always makes a bad situation worse.

Emotional illnesses are one of the most common of faery ailments. Do not try to get to the root of the issue, just recognize that an individual faery, or a group of faeries, cannot be rational when their emotions are revved up far beyond any problem you can see or they can tell you.

To begin your spell to soothe the faeries you will need tranquil music. Soft Celtic music, slow folk tunes, meditation music, and recordings by faery song writers, such as Gary Stadler, will all help the out-of-control emotions to shift downward. Of course, you have the choice of doing this in your own room, out in nature, or on the astral plane. The important part is that you do it and put all your will into the action.

Music has the power to switch our feelings back and forth across the emotions continuum for as long as we allow. As you get your inner balance and feel yourself centered in spirit, begin to project images of faeries participating in a moonlight party. There is no reason for this party. It is for fun, a celebration of the night and the energy of each nature spirit's joy in life.

By now you should begin to feel a tingling in the air around you. You and the fey are raising the vibrational rate of the environment. When you feel ready, either say the following, or put your own music to it. Don't be afraid to make music. Fey song is unique and rarely is performed the same way twice:

Dancing the circle for joy and pleasure,
Each spirit of nature is life's own treasure;
Drop all your worries and cease all your fears,
No sorrow is found in a faery's tears.
Dance for the night in praise of the moon,
Daylight shall break all too soon;
This is the moment to be carefree and wild,
No sorrow is found in a nature's child.
Dance to the woodlands, untouched and clean,
Sing to the woodlands for creatures unseen;
Until the sun rises, our revelry slips free,
As I will this, so mote it be!

You may find you want to stay nearby and watch the rest of the revelry, or even participate in it if you feel strong enough to know your limits. In a spell of this type it is difficult to get into a situation where you will be lost in faery with no memory of time or place. This spell is set to end when rays of sunlight fall on your natural dance floor.

Do be certain to check back again with the faery or faeries who needed your help to balance their mood. If you find there is still a pandemic of depression among the fey, you will need to repeat this spell for several nights, and also bring libations of milk, bread, honey, and a handful of energizing herbs to toss around so that energy can reach the nature spirits. Good choices are cinnamon, nutmeg, allspice, or bay leaf.

You will also need to talk to some of the faeries one-on-one to determine for yourself that there is a valid reason for the depression. For example, if one faery started the rumor that their natural habitat is in danger, find out if the rumors are true or not. You may not be able to stop the destruction of their homes, but you can help them learn to accept this by helping them relocate. Taking cuttings of the plants and moving them to a safer place will keep the fey alive in both of our worlds. Be prepared for some who refuse to leave. They will miss the nature they were a part of, but they have the astral world in which to live and play if they choose to remain alive.

Faery Healing Spell #2: Healing a Fey Injury
Faeries can sustain physical injuries from one of three sources:

1. A session of fisticuffs with another faery. With their sensitive dispositions, this is common.
2. Being the "game" of animals who see faeries clearly. Dogs are usually the protectors of faery, but cats more often enjoy faeries as prey.
3. Finding a hole within, missing parts, or broken limbs because someone ignorantly picked or cut down the host plant without warning or permission.

If you are a practitioner of any discipline requiring you to assess or transfer energy, the healing techniques will be easier for you. Reiki is an excellent healing talent to develop when working with the fey. There are many books explaining it and teaching it. Though it is not as ancient as some eastern healing arts, Reiki, a Japanese method of energy healing, is an excellent skill for a faery shaman to have.

Do not think that a spell that is performed as a shaman—more in the mind and with energy transference—is not as real as a spell where you gather oils, stones, herbs, or light candles and chant for hours. The faery shaman has his or her healing skills within all the time. Asleep, awake, or even caught off guard, the faery shaman can center him or herself, balance out their own energy, and begin giving it to someone else.

The trick in this, if that's a term you like, is that you do not use all your own energy reserves to send to others. You supplement your own energy by pulling ninety percent of it from the environment surrounding you. If you deplete your own energy stores every time you practice faery shamanism you will burn out fast and be of no use to the fey, and you could become dangerously ill yourself.

When a faery in nature, or in its own astral world, asks for your help, the best place to draw energy from is the earth beneath your feet. Mother Earth may be growing old and tired, but, as with any loving mother, she is available to help her children. You can also draw energy down from above you. This is very effective if you believe in a god or creator who lives somewhere above you. As a last resort you can ask the four elemental rulers to assist you.

Begin with deep breathing. As you inhale you must use all your powers of visualization to draw the appropriate healing energy into yourself. This is yet another art which cannot be adequately put into words. There aren't any that describe this energy loading correctly, and one person's explanation may leave another person with false impressions, not on purpose, but just because we all express our experiencing in the way we think is best, and it may never match anyone else's.

As with all magickal arts, healing included, visualization of the outcome and the manipulation of energy fuel the spell. All else is window dressing, catalysts to help the shaman focus, but the energy is in the shaman and not in the catalyst.

You will know when you are ready to begin transferring the built-up energy into your faery patient. Trust that you will. Some shamans feel a tingle from the energy, others experience a sense of kinetic power flowing through them.

When you are ready to send the healing, see it come from your palms or one of your chakras, going into the patient. Visualize the faery becoming whole again, fill in the missing parts. It's likely other fey in the area will be helping you. Once the faery you are assisting looks normal again and claims he or she is feeling good, admonish that faery to retreat into the astral. He or she needs to be as away from the physical world as possible to rest and get strong again.

There are no words needed for this spell, but many like to add something to feel there is closure to the work. Not all nature spirits can be revisited depending on your location. If you need a closure in words, try something such as:

> I bid you go to heal and rest,
> So you may return at your very best;
> Beloved of the earth, air, and seas,
> As I will it, so mote it be.

If you can revisit the faery in either the physical or astral plane, then do follow up to make sure that the injury was the only reason for the illness. The faery will also appreciate your concern and, in the future, be more willing to assist you in the healing arts.

11
Healing Holes in Your Spirituality

Something primal awakens in the human consciousness when we are separated from our cities and placed out where trees and animals outnumber us, where the noises of modern civilization are reduced. When we look up we see a dome of stars not usually visible to most of us.

In these settings we can hear the cries of wild animals, we can hear and see the faeries as they play around us. We hear the elementals of water and air, feel the heat of communal fires, and reconnect with earth. This connection to the land brings both humans and faery closer to deity. The spirits of people long gone also haunt these sacred grounds. Whether they lived a few hundred years ago or a few thousand, they are in spirit shamans seeking to work with the nature spirits to guard, guide, and support the land. Faery shamans honor the spirits of nature whose territory we inhabit, and we honor the elder spirits of the land.

Faeries in Ancient Religions

Because they are closer to nature, and on a level of the astral plane, faeries are closer than humans to the divine or the source of creation. Many of the pantheons of Gods and Goddesses worshipped today by seekers of the old ways were at one time or another "demoted" to the status of faeries by the early Church. Others were demonized. Today, some New

Age Judeo-Christians view the fey as the lowest caste of the angelic hierarchy, the ones on the plane closest to humanity who can help take our concerns and wishes to a higher power.

The best known of these deities (who are now often called faeries) are the Tuatha de Danaan of Ireland. The name roughly translates as the Children of the Goddess Dana, who has connection in lineage and aspects with the pan-Celtic/Britannic Goddess Brighid. When the final wave of continental Celts came to Ireland from Galicia (now western Spain) they were said to have encountered a race of very large and very bright beings ruling over the land. These beings were blonde, tall, strong, and beautiful to look upon, and they were said to possess power over the elements.

The old Irish Druidic poet, Amergin, is credited with composing a famous bardic poem he sang after the Celts—then called the Sons of Mil or The Milesians—first set foot on Irish soil, somewhere "in between," in the meeting of water and land (1500–500 B.C.E.). The poem, which in reality is a spell of conquest disguised as a song, has been translated many times into English and is well known among Pagans following Irish or Celtic-based traditions. Several popular Irish and Pagan singers have set the poem to music of their own because even though the beautiful words exist, the music has been lost. We know it today as "The Song of Amergin."

> *I am the wind that blows across the sea,*
> *I am the wave of the deep,*
> *I am the roar of the ocean,*
> *I am the stag of seven battles;*
> *I am the hawk perched on the cliff,*
> *I am the ray of golden sunlight,*
> *I am the greenest of plants,*
> *I am the wild boar on the hilltop;*
> *I am the salmon in the river,*
> *I am the lake on the plain,*
> *I am the word of knowledge,*
> *I am the point of a spear;*
> *I am the blade of the sword,*
> *I am that which rules the elements,*

I am the lure beyond the ends of the world,
I am a shapeshifter and I am God.

It is obvious Amergin and the Sons of Mil witnessed the Tuatha's control over the elements, which, in their earthbound world was the equivalent of divinity. Amergin's song was an attempt at magickally shifting that base of power from the Tuatha to the Druids and clan chiefs of the Celts.

This is magick similar to the song magick we discussed earlier. For the Celts, song had enough power to dethrone a king if that was the magician's will.

Folk stories continue to tell us that the Tuatha, who had only old bronze weapons, were finally defeated by the Celts who had learned to make iron tools in continental Europe. This time period marks the transition of Ireland from the Bronze Age to the Iron Age, according to anthropologists. The Tuatha went to hide underground in caves, stone raths, or earthen mounds. Even today many modern Irish believe the songs and revelries of faery can be heard near these mounds, particularly between the Spring Equinox and the Summer Solstice when faeries in Western Europe are thought to be more active and visible to humans.

Unlike most cultural pantheons, the Celts do not have one unifying creation myth. As a result we have a collection of rich stories to choose from, all of which may have once been part of a creation myth or myths. From these myths we can glean an idea of how an ancient people viewed this world and the otherworld, what traits they valued among their people, and how they expected their deities to behave and fit into their views on cosmology.

Folklore describes the powers that are most often associated with Gods and Goddesses; these include the fertility of the land, safe birth, honorable death, salvation from starvation, the bestowing of wishes in specific situations, and—always—control over the elements of earth, air, fire, and water. The quirky fact that faeries are still feared by many modern, intelligent, well-educated Irish is a testament to their once-held position as deities.

Connecting to the Divine by Connecting to Faery

As we've discussed before, there is a reason people are drawn to wild and spectacular nature, and the reason is we are closer to the rare power of our creator when we are there. Whispering a devotion to a personal deity while watching a hawk fly overhead, making a small stone medicine wheel in red rock country, or becoming one with the spirit of the stag in the forest are all ways in which we reconnect to deity. This is known as the art of mysticism.

Mysticism is a reaching out toward the creator, seeking to better understand and to become closer in spirit to that creator. We are pushing our energies outward, trying to transcend the earth plane to reach stop one on the journey: the plane of the nature spirits. Nature spirits can help us raise our own inner vibrational rate to ascend through their world and come closer to the creator. With their help we climb higher, drawing ourselves toward the essence of the divine.

On the other hand, magick is the process of pulling both divine and elemental energies inward, to be directed to a situation or a need we have in our physical lives. These are often issues of which nature spirits have no understanding, and, as much as they might want to help us, they don't have the skills in this area. This is when we ask the help of spirit guides and other types of faeries who lie beyond the scope of this book.

Regardless of what overall model of the universe we may hold, we all have our own ways of conceptualizing its planes. On our way up to the realm of the Gods and Goddesses we must first pass through the land of nature spirits and the world of faery itself.

As the Munchkins did for Dorothy and Toto in *The Wizard of Oz*, faery can see us safely to the end of their world as we attempt to ascend to greater spiritual heights. Enjoy this help. It will diminish as you ascend. Finding the creator is something we all have to do alone.

If you are interested in a composite, detailed analysis and how-to on ascension magick, I recommend Christopher Penczak's book *Ascension Magick: Ritual, Myth & Healing for the New Aeon* (Woodbury, MN: Llewellyn, 2007). Christopher goes beyond the realms of nature spirits and other faery to the "upper dimensions" where our minds are conditioned to believe we can find our creator.

Using Astral Projection and Faeries
to Heal Your Spirituality

One helpful trick the fey have taught me is astral projection. Using this form of remote healing I send out my conscious mind to some specific place where the elements are balanced in accordance with my goal and where I am safe from lower astral entities who may have negative intentions. If I visualize myself lying down in a bed of scarlet poppies or bright autumn leaves, and allow my essence to sink deep inside this place, eventually my mind travels to a place of spiritual learning. There are many books available on learning astral projection, including my own *Astral Projection for Beginners* (Llewellyn, 2002). If you are not familiar with this art, or wish to learn more, a quick trip to the metaphysical section of your local bookstore will yield many books about different techniques. One will work for you.

Preparations

Until you reach the point where you can project your consciousness outward, the next best thing is to sit or lie down. Begin taking slow, deep breaths; with each one, feel your mind slowing. If your mind drifts, don't get frustrated, just bring your thoughts back to your breathing. Then begin to visualize the "real you" looking down on the physical you from a few yards above your head. Eventually your mind will get the idea and you will be able to make it travel at will, even to the other side of the planet.

This sounds easy in theory, but it takes some self-discipline to master. The astral plane is also a great place to play, but to make these events work for you as a healer on an ongoing basis you must remember that you are a faery shaman and limit your play. Otherwise the fey will become accustomed to your sport and stop taking your vows of shamanism as a serious commitment.

Involving the Faeries

Because at least half of the healing energy you have available comes from faery, you must keep the majority of your astral time connecting to nature spirits by making yourself the center of an earth-based spiritual center.

The fey will join you in almost any healing effort if you ask them politely. In a special spot in nature—or nature on the astral plane—they may want to play first and work later. Gently remind them you are a faery shaman, and your work must come first. Reissue the invitation to have them work with you, and be certain your words are as polite as possible. Commands will only get you into big faery trouble, probably the most maddening hassle you will ever have to experience. Capriciousness and sensitive feelings are natural to them.

When you are out with the fey and have completed your healing rituals and spells, acquiesce to the faery need for play time. These are your partners in healing, why would you want to shun them for a social event? The trick to making this work is for you to tell yourself that you are in charge of what you do and for how long. Falling asleep during this play period has its pros and cons. In sleep it is easier to lose track of time, but it may also allow you to experience a profound bonding with the faeries. Remember, work first, then play. This balances your work and play and gains you the respect of the fey.

If you are on a spiritual quest needing a quick resolution and feel you have no time for play, then say so. Tell this to the nature spirits, to other helpful faeries, and to any spirit guides you may have. Ask the advice and help of the elemental rulers: the Gnome King (earth), the Sylph Queen (air), the Salamander King (fire), and the Undine Queen (water). This quartet has the ability to ascend beyond their own realm of existence just as we do, but it is more difficult to travel to a world removed more than one plane from our own, such as the higher astral worlds which take more energy and intent to enter. Make the trip worth their efforts.

The realm of faery is the closest to our known physical world. Thus, faeryland is more accessible to our psyches. Faery may lead us to the doorway to another plane, but they may or may not be able to take us through that door. This is why asking the help of the elemental rulers is crucial. If any being from faery can help you make this leap, it is the elemental rulers.

You can also use other non-faery models for ascension, such as the Tree of Life from the Kabbaltah. This is not an archetype the faeries understand. To gain spiritual ground with faery help you have to do it their way. There is nothing greater or lesser about how and where you travel, but the adventure of traveling the path to our creator is much more fun when the fey come with us. If we let our fey friends show us the way, we will also feel closer to the divine.

Healer, Heal Thyself!

Sometimes you may find you run across a client who's already skilled in meditation, energy healing, or other forms of natural healing. In such a case it is perfectly acceptable—even preferable—to allow that person to undergo the faery shaman meditation. The only adjustment you will need to make is that this person is not likely requesting to become a faery shaman. He or she just needs help with some healing, and often the fey know what we humans need better than we do.

Doing things for ourselves is much more empowering and much more successful than having them done for us. I got to watch this first-hand at a summer festival where I was a guest speaker in 2007. A man in my faery healing workshop had been injured while serving in Iraq four years earlier. His left hand had taken a spray of shrapnel, which damaged the nerves from the wrist down, numbing them from all sensation of touch or of heat and cold.

During the meditation he was holding the hand of his fiancée, and he gave her a little squeeze. Even knowing he could not feel her fingers, she squeezed back anyway. To his surprise he felt the pressure. The feeling was coming back in his little finger and the outside area of his hand. His son later came in and gave me a huge hug and thanked me. I told him I appreciated it, but it was his father and faery who did all the work.

Another woman reached the point in the meditation where she had to choose which elemental kingdom she wished to enter: earth, air, water, or fire. The elemental kings and queens told her she already was a faery shaman, and she already possessed her talisman identifying her as such. After the meditation she spoke with me to try and figure out what that meant.

She happened to mention that she loved hummingbirds and kept things around her house to attract them. A hunt ensued for a copy of Ted Andrew's much-referenced book, *Animal Speak*, a wonderful primer to the world of animal shamanism. The book is very popular, and it didn't take her long to find someone with a copy. She sat beside me and opened Ted's book to the place where he described hummingbirds as knowing which flowers are best used for healing. Their knowledge comes from their interaction with a flower's scent, color, and other chemical components. Ted wrote that the hummingbird can teach us "how to draw life essence" from the flowers and "create your own medicine." The woman's hummingbird talisman could teach her healing skills and be a conduit for bringing love into her life.

Another technique for self-healing is to nestle yourself in a garden, a patch of wildflowers, or a woodland, and just lie on the ground. Envision Mother Earth and her contingent of faeries ministering to your greatest needs. You don't even have to explain your need. Mother Earth knows her children and the fey will follow her.

If you work with stone energies—also faery energy—or with non-caustic essential oils, these can be placed on the body to bring both the energy of Mother Earth and faery closer to you. Traditional application sites are the wrists, the inner elbow, the arches of the feet, and the chakra points. A stone can pull out pain, and when it is placed back on Mother Earth, those illnesses and road blocks will be grounded into her, safely away from her cherished creations.

There are dozens of books on both the healing and magickal power of stones. Color, shape, clarity, and location all combine to make a stone's energy what it has become. A quick Internet search will give you some basic information on these stones, and will probably recommend easily obtainable stones for healing use. Charge them with faery energy by placing them in mother earth overnight. When you take them out, clean them under cool running water as you focus on the stone's healing purpose. Administering the healing can come through carrying the stones, wearing them, holding them, having them in a medicine bag, or by placing them in a specific location in or near your home. Let the fey be your guide as to the best use of a healing stone.

12
Healing the Physical Body

I know of no illness that cannot be treated with some measure of success with faery. Remember that "treated" is not synonymous with "cured." Treated means we can do things to ease the symptoms of a disease even if we cannot halt the progression of the illness. We can alleviate pain, soothe an itch, ease cramps, invigorate the tired, etc. This is also called treating the symptoms and not the disease. By cured we mean that our client is in a state of wellness and comfort in which no trace of disease can be detected even by the most sophisticated medical tests. More important, the client feels whole and well. But even licensed medical professionals have to deal with the frustration that some illnesses are not curable.

To do our best as faery shaman healers is to work with modern medicine to achieve the same healing goals, or to take preventive measures to protect our health. Never go it alone with any illness unless you are a licensed medical professional. Not only could you make a serious mistake, but the fines and jail time you would face for practicing medicine without a license are not worth it.

The Basics of Faery Healing for the Physical Body

Plants, herbs, flowers, and trees that have healing properties via either magickal or medical administration are legion, and it takes a skilled botanist, healer, or faery shaman to know precisely how to administer these remedies. As you grow as a shaman and an alternative healer, more information will be conveyed to you from plant spirits, and you will gain the confidence you need to be more effective in healing more illnesses. You may even find a licensed physician or pharmacist willing to talk to you about plants that cause allergies or that are contraindicated by medicines your patient is taking.

Profound wisdom, keen analytical thinking, and much study is required of the faery shaman who wishes to use his or her connection with faery to heal. This obligation is nonnegotiable once you've accepted the talisman of the shaman offered by faery, and it is not an easy path.

There are reasons why the medical profession requires extensive study, licensing, and continuing medical education for the rest of a doctor's career life. As with manufactured pharmaceuticals, dangerous interactions and allergic reactions can occur when using natural remedies. Repeat this mantra until you know it as well as your name: Just because it's natural does not make it safe!

Let us consider poison ivy. It's natural. It grows wild. It requires no patents, manufacturing, or distribution, but no one would call it "safe," and no one wants it on their skin or—worse still—inside their body. Ingesting the plant's leaves, or inhaling the smoke of burning poison ivy, can be lethal.

Administering Alternative Medicine

In earlier chapters we discussed some common medicinal plants and oils, their uses, side effects, and their dangers. If you are performing a healing for anyone but yourself, you need to know all you can about the illness and the health history of the person you are helping.

You will have to take notes on the illness. You will also need to go into faeryland once again, through the gates of the faery shaman, to consult with various plants and their spirits and listen to their suggestions.

You can do this in your own backyard if you wish to cultivate a garden of healing herbs. Many faery shamans do. Just remember the drawback is that each faery can only tell you how he or she can aid in healing. You may not have the best plant for your client in your garden. Even pharmacies don't keep huge inventories of every drug. In faeryland you'll find a huge array of plants to choose from and many faeries to help you decide which ones will be most beneficial. As you progress and grow in skills, you will have a better idea of what to keep on hand for clients.

Once you have selected a plant, or a combination of plants for healing, you must then decide on the method of administration. Until you have more experience it is wise to stick with those that do not come in contact with the skin and are not ingested. Like any professional, you must keep records of what you are doing to treat your client. This helps you to learn what plants work best for what illnesses and what plants do not work. It also gives you a record describing exactly what was done and when, should anyone challenge your methodology.

Faery Tales

A common method of healing in the fey-human partnership involves a form of aromatherapy. Choose a plant whose scent is a faery favorite (see the list given in Chapter 7). Place the live plant in the sleeping room of the ill person, so he or she can inhale the fragrance. Avoid plants that are toxic, however, even though some of these are loved by the fey.

Astral or Remote Healing with Faery

Take your astral body into the world of faery. Speak with the elemental rulers. Seek out totem plants, the ones with whom you feel a rapport, and talk to them about the illness you need to cure. Sometimes these "needs" are more magickal than medical, but faery can assist with that too.

The best time to do this is at night when there is less emotional static from the world around you to distract you from your goal. In faeryland, it can be any time of night or day you prefer. Keep your eyes open and your ears turned to the landscape of faery in case one small nature spirit calls to you, one who may have the answer you seek.

Some nature spirits cannot travel far from their plant home. There appears to be a radius they can move around in, but their souls seem attached to the living plant. Others can break off a part of their plant and give it to you. In either case, your goal is to get the nature spirit's energy to go with you, astrally traveling to the bedside of the person who needs healing or magickal assistance.

Listen to the faeries. They may know of a way you can carry them along with you. Stick to the faeries' instructions for removing, transporting, and returning them to their homes.

At the bedside of the sick person use your "twilight eyes" to assess the chakras. This means you look through the sick person, not at him or her. Some call this indirect sight, and you will find with practice that you become very good at looking at all sorts of beings and seeing the dark areas or imbalances in an energy field. Especially take note of any chakras that have dark spots; note any that are wide open or shut tight. Based on your patient's emotional and physical needs, the chakras may need to be cleaned, balanced, then set in their perfect positions. Listen to your faery allies. They have a sight we don't have, and they may see needs we cannot.

The same is true for the patient's aura, the etheric body that surrounds a living thing. Note if the colors are bright and clear; note holes or dirty spots. If the faery advises, you can project other colors into the person's aura to strengthen it and help your client heal.

Once that is done, allow the faery to go to work on the client with his or her own personal style of healing. Most nature spirits who come with me to sickbeds usually work on a body the same way a human energy healer would. They touch, send energy, move energy, massage, and cleanse the aura. As they do this I am able to see the change in the appearance of the person, and in his/her aura and chakras.

After the faery is done working, he or she may request you do other energy therapies. Don't try to be the big shot. Faery medicine is ancient. Trust that this nature spirit knows what he or she is asking of you.

The entire process may take thirty minutes or several hours. You will remain on duty until the faery says it is time to leave.

Before leaving offer thanks and a token of your appreciation to the faery for assisting you. Coins and shiny stones are favorite gifts. Tell the faery you will return to let him or her know how the client is doing, and, if necessary, make a second request for assistance. Then transport your faery spirit helper back home in the way it was requested.

By following these rules of basic courtesy, and treating the faery as your equal—an equal with much more experience than you have—you will find he or she is much more willing to help you the next time. Your reputation for procedure, courtesy, and adhering to the rules will spread, expanding the scope of the healing powers you have with faery.

Spells to Heal the Body

There is a never-ending debate about when, why, and how someone has the right to perform healing on or on behalf of someone else. In many natural spiritualities it is considered an invasion of someone's free will to heal without express permission. This works in most cases, when the one asking for healing is alert, participating, and not in critical condition.

By critical condition we mean an emergency situation, one in which life is at stake. Some would apply the word "emergency" to a situation where even quality of life is at stake. After more than a quarter century pondering this question, I have to agree with those who throw out the permission clause in a medical emergency. The reason? Medical personnel are bound by law and oath to save lives any way they are able and to worry about the consequences later. I believe this applies to the faery shaman.

If my car ever ran off the road and into a tree, rendering me unable to make decisions for myself, I hope someone would be supporting me with faery healing energy—including the faeries in that tree I just hit— until the paramedics could arrive. I would then expect the paramedics to do all in their power to resuscitate me and sustain my life until I could reach a hospital, where I would expect doctors and nurses trained in emergency medicine to take over and do the same thorough job.

The following healing spells are typical of those done within the fey-human partnership. For the beginning faery shaman, it is a good idea to take your first steps in spellwork from the books of others, tailoring them to the needs of yourself or your client. You'll know when you are ready to do more on your own, directed less by books and more by faery guidance. The best indicator that you're ready to solo is you will find your communication with faery becomes more cryptic.

Faery Alert

Faery will test you with riddles. They may tempt you with scents but not reveal the scents' names. They may allow you to peek at a flower without telling you the species. Faery expects its human shamans to be able to puzzle out the tough answers. If you can't follow their thought processes within a reasonable amount of time they will feel you're not clever enough to keep working with them. They may advise you to wait until your intuitive side catches up to your intellectual side.

If your calling is that of a faery shaman, you will rise to the challenge. After all, you've gotten this far. You know already that faery magick is hard work. It can also be fun and rewarding to watch how different things manifest through faery.

A Faery Diagnosis Spell

Use this technique when you have an ailment you don't understand or know how to treat. This spell is more difficult than most, and must be done astrally, in the world of faery. Keep in mind as you undergo this faery diagnosis that the faery world is made up more of feelings and emotions than blood and bone. Faery is excellent at finding destroyed emotions, broken trust, insecurity, spiritual gaps, and other things to do with mind and spirit. They are a lot less accurate when it comes to treating our physical bodies.

The fey do not seem to be vulnerable to certain physical illnesses, and consequently they are unfamiliar with ours. Once in a while I've had a faery tell me there seems to be inconsistent energy or a blocked area of energy near a particular internal organ. That is usually the source of the problem. It doesn't tell me everything I need to know, but it helps me narrow down my problem when speaking with my doctor, and it probably saves money on medical testing in areas where there is no problem.

On the mental and emotional side, faery can tell you what to say to your psychiatrist or therapist. This also saves money because faery cuts through all the clutter in your mind and gets to the heart of your problem. You may not like what you hear, and you may be uncomfortable talking about it, even with your doctor, but faery is almost always right in this area of your health.

To undergo a faery diagnosis of this type, present yourself again as a faery shaman, entering faeryland through the flaming gates. Go to the hilltop and tell the elemental rulers what it is you seek. Healing is a subject in which they have a great interest. I think part of that interest is because it helps them to better understand humans. Prepare to be questioned, and do not act agitated or offended by any of their inquiries. They will be using this information not just for their own learning, but to know where to send you in their world for diagnosis. Each time they get a human spirit to the right place, it helps the next one who comes along.

Often this process works best in the faery world, unless you have a garden or herb area you can lie in and not be distracted by insects and the sounds of the world moving about you. When you arrive inside the flaming gates, ask the first faery you meet where you need to go. She may tell you or escort you. Follow her instructions, and those of any other faery you meet along the way who already knows why you are in his world.

You will be asked to lie down in a thick bed of foliage. It may be autumn leaves, green grass, flowers, herbs, wildflowers, pine needles, etc. Whatever they choose will be comfortable and fragrant. This will allow the faeries to make a diagnosis. You will also be in a position to ground the sickness out of you, and absorb the positive and healthful vibrations of the foliage chosen for you. This way you still get some healing even if the fey are not 100 percent familiar with your ailment.

Spell for Breaking a Fever with a Faery Potion

For this spell you will need a cold washcloth, a basin, cooled water from boiled chickweed, a tea ball, and white willow bark tea. Make sure the client does not have problems taking aspirin. Because of the possibility of severe negative side effects, this potion should never be given to anyone under eighteen.

Chickweed can be bought at your local occult shop or online stores catering to metaphysical interests. With herb magick, less is preferable to large quantities. Remember it is the energy of the herb, not the amount, you need to use. Stop thinking like modern medicine tells you to think. Using something in a high dose or for longer than needed is usually not going to change the course of healing.

Boil about two tablespoons of the chickweed until it begins to break down. The common variety of this herb is soluble in water. Allow the mixture to cool, then strain out the remaining chickweed from the water. Pour the water into a large basin and refrigerate until it is just cool enough to be comfortable on the skin. You want cool, not cold.

Using a tea ball, cook but do not boil the white willow bark in another pan until a light colored tea is produced. The bark contains salicylic acid, which is also known as aspirin. Heating the water too high may damage some of the acid's effectiveness. Serve the tea warm to the patient.

After the tea has been consumed, have your client lie down. Wash his or her face, arms, legs, chest, and other exposed skin with the chickweed solution. Chickweed is a natural refrigerant and will help bring down the fever faster. As you wash the client, solicit the help of faery using the following request:

> Healing magick of the fey,
> I ask your help in here today;
> Cool the fever, break the fire,
> In (client's name) new health inspire.

Never use aspirin or any other product containing salicylic acid on children, especially when the precise diagnosis is unknown. The threat of Reyes' Syndrome is very real, and it can lead to liver failure and coma. Another threat is Samter's Triad Syndrome, also known as Aspirin Induced Asthma (AIA). Also, never give aspirin products to anyone who is taking blood thinners, who has a history of asthma, who might have chicken pox, or ulcers.

13
Healing the Home

The Basics of Faery Healing for the Home

Several species of faery make their home in your home, or your barn, fields, and any other outbuildings. Folklore tells us that when we are kind to these elven faeries they will do all they can to help protect us, our animals, and our homes. Libations of milk, honey, bread, or whiskey, left out each night for these faeries will solidify your partnership. The result is a happier home, one with less quarreling and fewer worries.

The fey can and will protect your home from the elements inasmuch as they are able. They are very good at redirecting lightning from your home and outbuildings, and can prevent fires before they start. They are less effective in deflecting dangerous weather, such as hurricanes, tornadoes, earthquakes, and floods, but they will do what they can to minimize any damage. They will also help you rid your home of unwanted energies or invaders both physical and astral.

The natural exuberance of house faeries to be playful and helpful will remain as long as you and your housemates show respect and offer thanks and gifts to them. They will also bring a lightness to a home darkened by arguments, grief, and personality clashes. If you have one particular housemate—and this includes your family—who seems troubled and refuses to seek psychiatric help, the fey can lighten the atmosphere so all who live under your roof can talk things out with greater ease.

Healing the home and those who dwell there is not something for which you often have to make a formal plea. House fey, like Brownies, House Gnomes, Beantighs, faeries of your hearth, and crop nature spirits, want the energy around your land in a positive state of balance because they live there too, and no one wants to stay in a home where every day and night is chaotic and uncomfortable.

Spells to Heal the Home

There are specific spells you can do with your faery partners to speed up positive change. They require lots of time and visualization, a good rapport with the local faery life, and little else other than the traditional libations.

Faeries who enjoy working around a house or farm will often take care of your animals, seeing to their needs, and warning you if something is about to go wrong. Listen with your mind and heart, not just your ears, and you will soon develop the ability to communicate with your house faeries in words.

Spells to Protect Your Home

One of the easiest ways to bring in a protective energy is to walk around outside while mentally projecting a need for which you have no solution. The fey will hear your thoughts if you concentrate on them. Sometimes you will hear an answer, or you might feel you've come up with your own answer when it is the house fey who have put a possible solution into your head. Even if you are certain you came up with a solution yourself, you should still give thanks to the faeries and offer them an extra libation or gift just in case you had their assistance without being aware of it.

The kitchen is today's hearth. You may not cook in a fireplace, but the stove is still the hearth and heart of your home. This is where all members of the household come to eat meals and share the day's news. Leave libations for the house fey near your stove at night and they will provide an atmosphere as peaceful as they are able.

If your concern is theft, allow your house faeries to make suggestions of flowers, herbs, and other methods of protecting your home. This is accomplished by placing the required item in all your windows and over your doors.

A popular protective practice is to wash your windows in water which has been infused with the essence of the common herb known as mugwort on a warm stove. You need very little of the plant, and only enough water to clean the windows. This will not only keep out burglars, but will also protect the thresholds to your home from unwanted astral beings or faeries who delight in causing discord.

Visualizing a Faery Star, a star with seven points instead of five, will protect anything it touches, including windows, doors, cars, rooms, animals, people, and unseen invaders. Some faery shamans visualize these stars being put into place, others use the common herb known as mugwort water or slightly salted water and actually draw Faery Stars on the doors and windows. If you're not sure what is best, ask your resident faeries for advice. Within a few days you will receive an answer. It may not be verbal, and it may come to you in a dream, but you will recognize the response when it comes because your subconscious mind has been looking for the answer and will make a lot of noise in your head until your conscious mind grasps the idea.

It is a good idea to erect a faery shrine somewhere in your home or on your land. This does not need to be large or elaborate. It need only be a resting place that is meant for the exclusive use and comfort of your local faeries. Because I do not share a bathroom with anyone else in my home, I've had the luxury of creating a faery shrine in there. Aside from photos, painted tiles, sculptures, and other artwork, I keep a small bowl containing special stones. I raided my own stone supply to find the prettiest ones to offer to the fey. Keep in mind that once something has been given as a gift to faery you cannot take it back or borrow it to use for some other purpose. You may be able to work out a trade with the fey, but they will expect an item of equal or greater value.

Even if you live in a small apartment you can set up some type of shrine for the use of your resident faeries in a small but demarcated area. Window gardens, near the stove, near a fireplace, or in a sunny room, will all please the fey. It also helps you obtain their respect so that your mutually beneficial partnership will continue.

The Faery Star Baby Blessing Spell

Everyone knows the story of "Sleeping Beauty," a princess born to a King and Queen much beloved in their kingdom. Faery godmothers came to bless the baby upon her birth. We are told one invitation was lost, and so the faery who didn't receive an invitation came to curse the child.

Baby blessing rites are still part of all religions in all cultures. These range from dedicating the child to live in a "godlike manner," to offering good wishes, to committing him or her to a lifetime of service to the religion or the community. Baptism is a familiar rite among Christians. In Paganism we most often hear this ceremony called a Wiccaning, but there are many other names for the rite among Pagans who are not Wiccans. What each ceremony shares is the offering of multiple blessings from clergy, family, friends, siblings, the ancestors, and the nature spirits.

For a true faery-style blessing we will use the image of the septagram, or the seven-pointed star many of us refer to as the Faery Star. It always sits with its top point up and two of the remaining six points pointing downward.

Who performs the blessing, or who shares in the blessing, whether this is an addition to other blessings, etc., is entirely up to the parents. The Faery Star Baby Blessing has eight parts, one for each point on the star and one more.

> *At the top of the star is the point of one,*
> *May your days be blessed with the warmth of the sun.*
> *We bless by the moon at point number two,*
> *So peace and second sight will be known to you.*
> *The gift of green is at the point of three,*
> *That the faery world shall always be open to ye.*
> *The blue-green beauty of the point of four,*
> *Blesses you with beauty, love, and more.*
> *May the euphoria of point number five,*
> *Make you happy each day to be alive.*
> *The point of six gives the blessings of much,*
> *Yet only you decide the value of such.*
> *Now we circle back to point number one,*

And we offer all other joys to be won.
May nothing you lack in spirit or form,
And may health and well-being be a mantle worn.
Always here, on the star at point one.
And now we announce, and to the Gods we plea:
(This is the point at which the parents whisper the Craft name
of the child, the one they wish to give him or her until the child is old
enough to choose his or her own. The priest or priestess, or other elder
giving the blessing continues.)
_____ (child's name), known to the Gods shall be.
Protested and safe, by the faery charm,
That this child shall never come to harm.
So by the power of earth, moon, and sun,
Completing our circle, our spell is done.

Faery Garden Consecration

Many seekers who work closely with faery like to keep a garden of flowers and herbs that are pleasing to them, or that can be used for faery magick and healing. The garden's size and shape are up to you, and may be dictated by space restrictions. If you have room for only a few flower pots, that's fine. If you have a private yard where you can make a faery garden in the shape of the septagram, or Faery Star, that is terrific.

As you prepare the soil and plant your seeds or transfer flowers, hum a faery tune, and keep the purpose of your garden in your mind. You are making a garden that will be a place for faery to linger and play, as well as for you to enjoy and use.

When you have the garden completed, consecrate it to the fey by sprinkling it with water, sparkle dust, and glitter. As you spread each, speak words of dedication:

On the garden I sprinkle the water of life,
So faery life here may be healthy and rife.
I sprinkle the shimmering faery dust,
Which shows the fey a home here is a must.
I toss some glitter just for fun,
So our spirits in joy may meet here as one.

You may also decorate your garden with other whims, such as lights which are solar powered and will glow in the garden all night. Glow-in-the-dark butterflies, stars, or faery figures are a nice touch. Statuary is a perfect addition. Many people place whimsical statues in their gardens. Trust that a few garden faeries will not "out you" as a Witch if you're still in the broom closet.

If you have a tree near the garden, you can decorate it to please the faeries, just be careful not to hurt the tree. Anything tied onto the tree should be loose so that the branch can continue to grow. Tying decorations on with knitting yarn is best. After a few seasons of outdoor exposure, yarn decays and falls off on its own. Be vigilant and pick up the debris so birds and pets don't mistake it for food and choke on it.

Colored eggs, shiny stones, flowers, items covered in glitter, pieces of jewelry, coins, and food and drink libations will delight the faeries who choose to live in your yard. One day you may even find a strange shiny stone near your back door—a gift of thanks from the faeries. Whatever it is, put it on your altar, or some other place of honor in your home to please them.

Think of your garden as an ongoing faery shrine. Add a place to put offerings, and put little faery houses in small spots hidden under the foliage. You will be surprised at how many times you change your mind about what you plant, how to decorate, and where you align objects. The more you feel these urges, the closer you are becoming to the fey who make this garden part of their world-in-between-the-worlds home.

May you, as did I when I was an enchanted six-year-old, look out into your garden some spring night and be blessed and awed by the sight of the faeries dancing and singing in the garden you made and dedicated in their honor.

Spell to Find Prosperity: Need vs. Desire

The home is the seat of prosperity. It is where you come together with family and friends, where you share food, and where you laugh and cry with one another. In virtually all spiritual contexts the home is ruled by the element of earth, which is also connected to abundance and prosperity.

Purchasing or renting a home is easy, but none of us would argue that it takes money to keep a household going. A spell is not going to get you your dream home complete with stables, tennis courts, a sauna, three swimming pools, and a bridal path. Magick works based on need, not on desire only. Desire provides the energy you need to manifest a prosperity spell, but it will never bring you more than you really need. This is why magickal religions believe there is enough abundance in the world for all of us. When we each get what we need and are comfortable with it, the normal person loses the desire to push onward. To be obsessed with collecting more than one needs is greed, an attribute not rewarded by the universe or practitioner of magick.

Also, before we can launch ourselves into a prosperity spell with faery, we must deal with the great discrepancy in the definition humans and fey have of this word. To us it usually means material comforts that can be purchased with sufficient money. To faery it means having a strong connection to spirit and having all your vital needs met. Nothing more, nothing less. Which aspect of prosperity are we seeking?

Fairy tales about a pot of faery gold at the end of the rainbow have been misinterpreted by humans to mean material gain. The cauldron is a symbol, and archetype, of the womb of the mother Goddess who gave us birth. It is to her we shall return when this life ends so that we can be reborn from her. The riches of the cauldron are spiritual, not physical, which is why all the glitter, gold, and glitz of the world of faery can never be brought back to this world in the form we see it there. What we bring back is internal wealth, not external riches.

Faery prosperity spells are based on need and not desire. The fey will help you get a happy family, a peaceful home, food on the table, meaningful work to pay the bills, and some extra so that life can be enjoyed. If you're looking for an extravagant Hollywood mansion or a penthouse in Manhattan the fey cannot help you.

When asking for prosperity from faery, keep in mind that the fey operate on the barter system. You cannot trick them into believing something is of value when it is not. If you seek their assistance, you'll have to be willing to trade in return.

Seek out a quiet spot in nature, or in your own faery shrine at home, and take your offering to the faeries. Sit comfortably there for as long as you like. It does not matter if this is a day or night event, just so you feel safe and connected to faery. Begin talking with them, explaining your need. Ask for any help they are able to give. Let them know you will be looking for their answer even in your dreams. Give them your offering, then thank them for listening to you whether they can help you or not.

In many ways, communicating with the fey is the same as the way you speak to a cherished friend. You never discount the advice and you never put yourself in a superior position. In other ways, communicating with the fey is like prayer. You are asking for help, guidance, and comfort from someone in an unseen world. Trust your faery partners. Trust yourself.

An Afterword and a Wish

Good Luck on Your Journey, New Faery Shaman Initiate

This is just your beginning, my fellow faery shaman. There are no limits to how far this journey with faery can take you. There are many more mysteries to learn, many new levels of initiation to conquer, new techniques to master, and libraries of new understanding to grasp. The faery will help you as long as you remain committed to doing the work. The bibliography in the back of this book can give you the names of books that will help you go from a beginning faery shaman to one who moves through many worlds with ease and familiarity, accomplishing great wonders for those who ask for your help.

The world of faery is tricky and slippery, but that is part of its allure, the essence of something known but never fully known that keeps us coming back for more of their energy. Majestic, tragic. Wild, melancholy. Helpful, playful. Faery is all these things and more, and it is a world you will be glad you entered.

Be proud of your accomplishments so far, new faery shaman. Be willing, strong, and courageous. May the sacred miracles of faery ride at your side, may their healing melodies play in your ear, may all their doors eventually open to you, and may all your healings be successful!

Appendix A: Online Resources

The online resources listed in this appendix were accurate to the best of my knowledge at the time this book was written. There are thousands more sites about faeries, magick, and nature spirituality to explore. I list the ones I am most familiar with, but this does not mean I share the point of view of each website owner. I do list some sites of faery artists who are gaining recognition for their work because I like and happen to own some of their work. This in no way implies that other artists are not just as talented, or that their websites are not just as lovely.

If you don't own a computer, most libraries and some public universities have machines you can use for specified allotments of time. You can get a free e-mail address through Hotmail or Yahoo, and you can register for payment services like PayPal, at no cost. This is simply the way business is now conducted by many stores, even if they still have a bricks and mortar presence. Many suppliers no longer produce printed catalogs for mail order.

If a link is not working, try using your favorite Internet search engine to find the new address. There are literally more than a million sites pertaining to the New Age, alternative healing, Eastern medicine, energy work, Paganism, Witchcraft, Wicca, magick, faeries, traditions, astral travel, lucid dreaming, jewelry, music, fine art, dietary healing, and the paranormal, and I could only provide space here for some of the largest and most popular.

This means you have a lot of information out there from many different points of view to think about as you choose your path through this life. Visit many sites, buy with care, read critically, but balance the critic inside by keeping an open mind. As many traditions advise, take what works for you and set the rest aside.

Please try to find things you want from merchants in your own locality before using mail order. They provide a valuable source of information, networking, and events at the local level, and we owe them as much support as we can give. It will be returned to us threefold.

About.com: Alternative Religions, Symbols: *altreligion.about.com/library/glossary/symbols/bldefswiccasymbols.htm*

Amy Brown Statuary: *www.amybrownsignatureseries.com*

Ancient Wisdom Herbs: *www.ancient-wisdom-herbs.com*

Angela Jarma, Fairy Actress: *www.funtasticparties.us*

Angelfire: *www.angelfire.com/home/thefaery6/index.html*

Art of Renae Taylor: *www.renaetaylor.biz*

Astroarcheaology: *www.archaeoastronomy.com*

Avena Botanicals: *www.avenabotanicals.com*

Azure Green: *www.azuregreen.com*

Blue Moon and Stars Magickal Jewelry: *www.bluemoon-inc.com*

Blue Pixie Faerie Art Gallery: *www.geocities.com/Area51/Lair/4042/Faerieart.html*

Brian Froud Fairy Art: *thepixiepit.co.uk/fairyart/brian_froud.htm*

British Pagan Circle: *www.geocities.com/RainForest/canopy/7046*

Chifaes: Other Faerie Links: *www.geocities.com/faeriechicago/faelinks.html*

Circle Magazine: *www.circlesanctuary.org*

Collected Pagan Resources: *www.pagansunite.com*

Collectible Fairy Dolls: *www.fairyvillage.com/c143/Collectible-Dolls180.html?FAIRYVIL*

Cottage of the Hedgewytch: *www.hedgewytchery.com*

Counsel of Setanta: The Faery-Faith Red Branch: *www.faeryfaith.org*

Crescent MoonGoddess: *www.crescentmoongoddess.com*

The Crucible Catalog: *www.crucible.org*

CyberMoon Emporium: *www.CyberMoon.us*

Dark Side Wiccan Resources: *www.americanwicca.com/dark-and-evil-witchcraft.html*

Digital Faery Art from the Netherlands: *www.elphame-art.nl/index2.php?taal=en*

The Druidic Clan of Dana: *www.faeryfaith.org/dcd.html*

Educate Yourself's Natural Healing Therapies: *www.educate-yourself.org*

E-Faires.com: *www.eFairies.com*

E-Witch Pagan Auctions: *www.e-witch.com*

The Enchanted Art of Jessica Galbreth: *www.enchanted-art.com*

Enchanted Woodland Faeries: *www.enchanted.co.uk/woodland.html*

Faerie, Faerie, Faerie Link: *www.katyberry.com/Rosepetal/links.html*

The Faerie Chronicles: *www.faeriechronicles.com*

Faerie Festival at Sproutwood: *www.faeriefestival.net*

Faerie Gathering Faerie Links: *www.thefaeriegathering.com/artist/links.html*

Faerie Journals: *www.faeriejournals.com*

Faerie Links: *www.nomenus.org/rflinks.html*

Faerie Magazine: *www.faeriemagazine.com*

Faerie Magick: Our Favorite Faery Links: *www.faeriemagick.com/links/links.htm*

The Faerie Patch: *www.thefaeriepatch.com*

Faery Faith Network: *www.faeryfaith.org*

The Faery Realm: *members.tripod.com/%7Efaery_queen/janet.htm*

Faerie Collectibles on Squidoo: *www.squidoo.com/Faeries*

The Faerie Realm KY: *groups.yahoo.com/group/TheFaerieRealmKY*

The Faeriewolds Festival: *www.faerieworlds.com*

Faerietail: Accessories for Your Inner Pixie: *www.faerietail.com/links.php*

Faerie Glen Newsletter: *www.faerieglenNJ.com*

Faerie Rings: *www.faerierings.com*

The Faerie Trail: *faerietrail.squarespace.com*

Fairy Photography by Margaret Dean: *www.fairyphotographs.com*

Fairy Statues from The Pyramid Collection: *www.pyramidcompany.com/42.htm*

Fantasy Art by Nene Thomas, Inc.: *www.nenethomas.com*

Fantasy Art by Patricia Rose: *www.patriciarosestudio.com*

Fantasy Art Gallery: *www.fantasygalleryart.com*

Favorite Faery Links: *www.sacredgrove.com/1favorite_faerie_links.htm*

Feri Trad (Her Circles): *www.witchcraft.co.il/circles/feri.html*

Feri Tradition of Victor Anderson: *www.geocities.com/Athens/Rhodes/5569/Faery_Trad_Intro.html*

For Faerie Lovers: *www.glisteningpixie.com/Faerie%20links.htm*

The Galleries of Peter Stone: *www.peterstone.com*

Greenbelt Green Man Festival: *www.greenbeltgreenmanfestival.org*

H-pathy: Homeopathic Medicine Information: *www.hpathy.com*

Healing Using Natural Home Remedies: *www.homemademedicine.com*

Herbal Magick, Inc.: *www.herbalmagickinc.com*

Herbs2000.com: *www.herbs2000.com*

Herbs 4 Healing: *www.herbs4healing.com*

Hobbyhorse Café: *www.hobbyhorsecafe.com*

Homeopathic Remedies: *www.homeopathiclaboratories.com*

I Believe!: *mysite.verizon.net/vzeppqi7/links/faeries.html*

The [Carl] Jung Page: *www.cgjungpage.org*

Lacie Lady's Collectibles Shop: *www.laceylady.com*

La Dolce y Vito Natural Body Care: *www.ladolceyvito.com*

Leydet Aromatics (essential oils): *www.leydet.com*

Magickal Education Convocation: *www.convocation.org*

Magickal Jewelry and Talismans: *www.magickaljewelryandtalismans.com*

Maryland Faerie Festival: *www.marylandfaeriefestival.org*

Medicinal Herbs and Nutraceuticals: *www.merck.com*

Moon Scents: *www.moonscents.com*

Mountain Rose Herbs: *www.mountainroseherbs.com*

My Witch Shop: *www.mywitchshop.com*

The Music of O'Carolan: *www.mandolincafe.com/news/publish/mandolins_00594.shtml*

Mystic Auction: *www.mystic-auction.com/cgi-bin/as/auction.pl*

The Mystic Cauldron: *www.mysticcauldron.com*

The Mystic Merchant: *www.mysticmerchant.com*

Mythic Journeys: *www.mythicimagination.org*

The Natural Remedies Encyclopedia: *www.pathlights.com/nr_encyclopedia*

New Age Information Network: *www.newageinfo.com*

newWitch Magazine; e-mail address: *info@newwitch.com*

The Old Ways: *www.oldways.com*

Pagan and Craft Traditions: *www.paganpath.com/trad.html*

Pagan Education Network: *www.bloomington.in.us/~pen*

The Pagan Federation, Canada: *www.pfpc.ca*

PanGaia Magazine: *www.pangaia.com*

Pagan Shopping: *www.paganshopping.com*

Paranormal & Parapsychology Listings: *www.theshadowlands.net*

POTO/"Procurer of the Obscure": *www.SacredSource.com*

R'chel Enterprises Stormsong Online Pagan Superstore: *http://store.stormsong.org*

Renaissance Faire Pictoral Fairy Links: *www.renaissancefairepictorial.com/fairies/fae_links.html*

Renaissance Magazine: *www.RenaissanceMagazine.com*

The Robin's Hood: *www.robinshood.org*

Sacred Isle: *www.sacredisle.com*

Scaerie Faerie Tails: *www.scaeriefaerietails.com*

Solitary Path Resources: *www.solitary-pagan.com*

Stonefence Photography: *www.stonefencephotography.com*

Stones of Avalon (Canadian Magazine); e-mail address: *stonesofavalon@hotmail.com*

Stregheria: Italian Witchcraft: *www.stregheria.com*

Tales of Faerie, Links: *www.talesoffaerie.com/links.htm*

Time of the Faeries by J Corsentino: *www.timeofthefaeries.com*

Top 50 Fairy Pages: *www.ultimatetopsites.com/entertainment/fairysara*

The Truth About Faeries: *www.faeryfaith.org/faeries.html*

Valley of the Sun: *www.sutphenpublishing.com*

Victorian Faery Paintings: *www.endicott-studio.com/gal/galvctf.html*

Wicca for the United Kingdom: *www.wiccauk.com*

The Wiccan and Faerie Grimoire of Francesca De Grandis: *www.well.com/user/zthirdrd/WiccanMiscellany.html*

Wiccan Resources Megasite: *www.americanwicca.com*

Wise Woman's Herbals: *www.wisewomanherbals.com*

Witch Market Auctions: *www.witchmarket.com*

The Witches' Voice (covers many occult interests): *www.witchvox.com*

Wizard's Junction: Faerie Links and Resources: *www.midnightenchantment.net/junction.htm*

The World of (Brian) Froud: *www.worldoffroud.com*

World Mysteries—Natural Healing: *www.world-mysteries.com/sci_15.htm*

Appendix B: Common Healthy Herbs and a Few Hidden Dangers

The faery shaman, like any alternative healer, must always remember the magickal properties of an herb or its oil are not always the same as its medicinal properties. Many herbs, even the benign ones, and their oils should never be used medicinally at all. Some contain parts that are benign and parts that are poisonous. If you are healing animals you must never forget we have different biological systems. What is a benign substance for humans could impair or kill an animal. One excellent book that will help you understand and use essential oils safely is Julia Lawless's *The Illustrated Encyclopedia of Essential Oils* (Shaftesbury, Dorset, UK: Element Books, 1995). The book is not oriented toward the magickal use of herbs, but it does discuss folk uses of the oils and the healing properties and precautions when using them. The companion book, David Hoffman's *The Complete Illustrated Holistic Herbal: A Safe and Practical Guide to Making and Using Herbal Remedies* (Shaftesbury, Dorset, UK: Element Books, 1996), is another excellent study guide.

As you read through this listing, make notes on the items you'll want to have on hand for emergencies, such as having a chest poultice ready for chest congestion. Some may already be in your kitchen, others you will have to buy from a specialist. Links to sellers are listed in the online resources Appendix A in this book.

Keep in mind that you are a faery shaman novice and you are not qualified to implement more specific techniques of energy healing. Unless you've been through classes to learn and be certified in energy healing arts such as Reiki, Rolfing, massage therapy, or other alternative healing methods, or if you do not have a valid medical license, you can end up facing steep fines and even prison time.

Use the information in this and any other books on faery healing with the goal of getting the best results possible for your client without stepping into areas where you are not qualified. Do not ever forget your partnership with faery. Acknowledge their assistance and support or you risk losing their friendship and assistance. They have the ability to make your life miserable for as long as they hold their grudge.

Be willing to err on the side of caution until you are an expert herbalist or can be supervised by a doctor and/or an expert herbalist. Your faery contacts can also advise you, and they also tend to err on the side of caution. Humans and faeries are just now reestablishing their former partnerships, and neither wants to do anything to put that relationship at risk.

Use astral or remote healing if you and your faery companion have any desire to work with one of these herbs. Even then, you are still dispensing the plant's energy into another's body. Use caution and common sense! Part of common sense is knowing that any plant that is too dangerous to be given physically can be given through hands-on energy transfers or in remote healing. Be creative; your clients will need your cunning.

The following list describes uses for common herbs, along with standard cautions and safety recommendations:

Alfalfa: aids indigestion, but too much alfalfa disrupts the body's red cell production.

Aloe: heals burns, sunburns, and provides relief for dry skin and some types of rashes. Apply a thick paste of the aloe to a burned area and let it dry. Check it again when dry, and if the skin is still warm to the touch, reapply until skin is cool. Mostly used topically. Can cause uterine contractions and should not be used by pregnant women.

Allspice: use sparingly in aromatherapy to produce a pleasant disposition and ease worries.

Angelica: can cause photosynthetic skin reactions when exposed to sunlight or ultraviolet light; fresh roots and seeds are potent poisons.

At one time angelica was made into a substance similar to chewing tobacco, believed to give the chewer immunity to illness. It works as a cough suppressant, but so do many other herbs without the risk of exposure to toxins. Similar in appearance to other toxic herbs, do not self-harvest unless you are an expert herbalist.

Anise: treats insomnia and dyspepsia. Anise and licorice are not the same thing, and the FDA notes this distinction. Anise is generally considered safe for consumption but testing shows there may be a link between licorice consumption and several types of hormonal and neurochemical imbalances.

Apple: soothes through transitions, a calmative. Apple juice is a general tonic, but apple seeds contain deadly cyanide.

Asafetida: expectorant, decongestant, wards off unwanted animals.

Basil: caustic and contains estrogens; raw herb or powdered herb good in protective rites.

Bay Leaves: contains estrogens; putting one in each window of your home wards off evil and jealousy.

Bittersweet: strong, often fatal, poison.

Boneset: as the name suggests, it was once believed to help broken bones knit properly. There is still controversy over the safety of boneset.

Broom: some varieties are poisonous and should not be used except in energy work (Reiki, meditation, remote healing, etc.) if you are not a doctor.

Buckthorn: poisonous and a possible carcinogenic; rumors of its internal cleansing powers are true only if you want to spend the night purging in a hospital.

Butterbur: use the powdered herb in capsules to ward off migraines.

Camphor: has a wide reputation as an aromatic or ointment because it is believed to loosen chest congestion and helps open blocked sinuses.

In truth, camphor can interfere with breathing and bring on asthmatic attacks. The hot oil is a deadly poison and should never be inhaled. Consult a pharmacist or doctor before using.

Cassia: one of the most caustic of the essential oils; contains protective and beautifying energies.

Catnip: a mild sedative found in many prepackaged calming teas.

Cedar: use the incense or the needles in a sachet for prosperity and abundance.

Chamomile: a cousin of ragweed. Anyone allergic to ragweed, or subject to "hay fever" should not use this. For some people this herb is relaxing and aids in digestion.

Clary Sage: helps ease attacks of asthma; mild pain reliever.

Cream of Tartar: for dyspepsia, nausea, and general stomach ailments. When cream of tartar ferments it produces sulfites, just like those found in wines and other fermented products. Those with serious allergies to sulfites or sulfa drugs should be cautious when using cream of tartar, or avoid it altogether.

Cypress Leaves: work as a topical coagulant. Do not use internally.

Damiana: speeds metabolism and sex drive, but is cardioactive and should never be taken in large amounts or by people with high blood pressure or other cardiovascular illnesses.

Dandelion: dandelion teas and wines are popular home remedies. Their young leaves have a mild narcotic affect that can ease pain; the roots and leaves are rich in vitamins A, B, C, and G.

Dill: brings wealth when worn into the faery world. Taken internally dill can cause uterine contractions.

Elder Tree Leaves: have been used as a poultice, cough syrup, and a tea to treat colds and flu. Too much is toxic. Consult an expert herbalist or doctor before using.

Eucalyptus: oil is poison, buy cough drops! You can also melt minute amounts of the oil into a large base of petroleum jelly to make a chest poultice. Do not try to ingest the oil without medical supervision.

Feverfew: as its name suggests, it is given as a tea to reduce fevers.

Forget-Me-Nots: poisonous, but can assist in faery glamour spells when used astrally.

Foxglove: once believed to help heart patients, but is in reality a cardioactive poison that can cause heart arrhythmia or failure.

Geranium: eases all stress conditions from tight throat to tension headaches, and the scent is relaxing.

Ginger: speeds metabolism and boosts body temperature to assist in weight loss, but can irritate stomach. Capsules are available, but are very harsh. Get your ginger in foods instead. Faeries love ginger for its capacity to create unexpected events they find humorous.

Ginkgo Biloba: a popular anti-aging and memory herb. May also counteract some of the side effects of certain antidepressants. Check with a doctor before adding this to your regimen.

Goldenseal: tea has been used for a myriad of minor health complaints, but may cause swings in blood pressure and uterine contractions.

Gotu Kola: has been used to help heal wounds and improve circulation, but should not be used by the novice faery shaman because of serious blood vessel concerns. May produce serious rashes and may be linked to skin cancers.

Hawthorn: a favored faery tree that is poison. Faeries do not appreciate humans taking pieces of hawthorn wood or flowers without permission.

Hyacinth: mood adjuster, sedative. There is evidence to suggest the smell of hyacinth is erotic to some people.

Hyssop: stimulates the circulatory system, good for arthritic pain, often used in teas as a general tonic.

Jasmine: used in healing of mind, stopping bad dreams, and inducing prophetic dreams. The night-blooming variety—one of 250 varieties in the world—is a faery favorite with a heady scent. Also used for faery love and beauty magick.

Lavender: another oil to relieve stress. Has mild antiseptic qualities and can be used on bare skin if it is diluted with a benign oil or a lotion.

Lemon: used in magick for employment, prosperity, and joy. Studies have shown people do more productive work and stay better focused when they smell lemon. Lemon juice is often put into expectorants with honey to treat a cold or flu. Even though lemon juice has gone through periods of being known as a fashionable hair lightener, the oils in the juice and rind can cause photosynthetic reactions on skin in sunlight.

Lemon Verbena: calms the digestive and nervous systems.

Lettuce: the juice of boiled lettuce leaves brings on sleep and helps reduce pain. Contains natural opiates and can cause dangerous interactions with other medicines. Talk with a physician before using. Needless to say, eating lettuce will not give you an opium buzz. Long live the salad!

Lily of the Valley: the scent of the flowers are soothing, but should never be burned for aromatherapy. All parts of the plant are strong poisons. Do not risk having Lily of the Valley in your home or healing clinic if pets and children are around.

Lime: excellent in spells of protection or to turn back negativity on one who has sent it to you.

Meadowsweet: tea has sometimes been used as a calmative, but other herbs taste better. This herb is deemed a carcinogen.

Mistletoe: once used in Europe to make a variety of medicines, the drawback is that many parts are poisonous, dosage must be controlled, and all of the plant must be kept out of the reach of children and pets. The folklore that mistletoe is an aphrodisiac is exaggerated.

Marjoram: may be used sparingly in spells for prosperity and inner peace.

Mullein: soothing in teas, a well-known faery herb that can help you see the Wee Ones. The seeds of mullein are poisonous and the dried herb contains tannins linked to stomach cancers if used in excess.

Mustard: it's not just folklore, this herb works wonders as a hot poultice for chest congestion.

Myrrh Gum: caustic and poisonous; use sparingly in aromatherapy to force the mind in productive and creative directions.

Nettle: common allergen that has no healing properties worthy enough to validate its use.

Nightshade or Belladonna: strong and fatal poison!

Nutmeg: most people are surprised to know this common kitchen herb is poisonous. A single clove can kill an adult. Some websites mention nutmeg can be fatal, including *www.mdidea.com/products/proper/proper074.html*. Rodale's *Herbal Home Remedies* states that large amounts of clove are fatal. In *The Illustrated Encyclopedia of Essential Oils*, the author mentions the substance myristicin, an halucenogen found in nutmeg. A mild narcotic but a strong emetic. Some pharmacists believe that the low death rate from nutmeg poisoning is because the body expels the poison in violent and prolonged sessions. The scent of the ground herb can stimulate your brain through a sluggish period. It also helps our general disposition, possibly a side effect of it being used in many holiday recipes.

Oleander: a deadly poison! If it grows in your yard and can be reached by pets or children, have it removed by a professional landscaping service.

Orange: use diluted oil to ease a tight chest or to soothe bouts of nausea; can be an invigorating scent.

Orange Blossom: the oil is costly, but very safe, and is a faery favorite. It can be used on skin to ease joint pain or reduce the appearance of scars when used as a paste. The scent gives those around it a calm but euphoric sensation. This is one of the least toxic of all plants, and has a low rate of side effects, though allergy sufferers may want to use caution.

Parsley: will clean your breath and help clear your palate. In quantities greater than a small sprig it is a diuretic and poison that can cause kidney failure.

Passion Flower: forget any images the mind comes up with for this one, it's poison.

Patchouli: a calmative and a stimulant—dose with caution until you know how your patient will react; grounding, germicide.

Peppermint: the oil is poisonous, buy the candy instead. Most mints have no actual taste. Their smell triggers what we perceive as taste. Gentle peppermint can have miraculous effects on an upset stomach.

Pleurisy Root: makes a good winter decongestant when used in a chest poultice.

Pomegranate: popular fertility aid.

Psyllium: seeds regulate movements of the large intestine. It can cause allergic reactions or block esophagus leading to asphyxiation. May also cause uterine contractions.

Queen Anne's Lace: a common allergen, but the seeds were used for two centuries by women in the southern Appalachian Mountains as a "morning after" pill. Obviously, the seeds contain some potent hormones. Also used in healing a mind that does not know what it wants. Consult a pharmacist or doctor before using.

Red Clover: used in teas for stamina because of its high iron content. Can induce a mild euphoria. Also contains estrogens.

Rose: used for skin eruptions and soothes stomach pain. Petals contain Vitamin C, overdoses can upset lymphatic system.

Rosemary: the oil is toxic and caustic. Some people use the oil to anoint candles. If you do, wash your hands thoroughly afterward and do not touch mucus membranes, particularly the eyes. Studies have shown rosemary is linked to hypertension and seizures. Use the energy of the needles for all types of healing, love magick, psychic and physical protection, concentration and focus, courage, or past-life work. Can be burned in small amounts as an incense, though some people find the smell unpleasant.

Spearmint: use the teas ready-made. This is soothing to the stomach and central nervous system.

Saffron: an expensive herb no longer available commercially in the United States; causes uterine contractions and possible birth defects.

Sage: common allergen, can cause breathing problems, but is an excellent and popular purification incense for any indoor space.

Sweet Pea: use oil or incense in healing broken hearts, providing hope, and as a light aphrodisiac. Placed in bath products it stimulates the skin to be more more receptive to tactile sensations.

St. John's Wort: parts of plant are poisonous, its use as an antidepressant is more hype than help.

Sandalwood: decongestant, mild antidepressant, anti-nausea, tranquilizing as an incense. Also a good glamoury perfume base. Burn the red wood chips for a peaceful environment. The scent of sandalwood will also raise the vibrational rate of any place it is used.

Scullcap: tea is used as a sedative, but the FDA deems it an undetermined poison. Try catnip or valerian root instead.

Skunk Cabbage: narcotic, but a strong diuretic; risk of severe dehydration. Avoid!

Tea, Black and Brown Varieties: soothes skin irritations and reduces swelling on the skin. Contains both caffeine and tannins. Research on British verses Middle Eastern tea drinkers noted far fewer cases of stomach cancers in Britain where tea is customarily served with milk.

Tea Tree Oil: helps break up congestion. This is a cure for minor skin and scalp ailments, and mixed with other oils or lotions to lessen its strength. It tingles, but is safe to place on bare skin.

Common Healthy Herbs and a Few Hidden Dangers

Thyme: caustic on skin and the oil is poisonous. Use only in externally scented healing charms for love, well-being, and undiagnosed abdominal upsets. NEVER use internally in medicinal proportions. Warn clients not to handle it.

Turmeric: potent diuretic, can damage kidneys. Use in sachets for healing a broken spirit.

Valerian Root: strong sedative that can be taken as a tea or in capsules. Is addictive and toxic only in large or prolonged doses. Do NOT use for aromatherapy. Because it has some genuine medicinal uses, it is included here. As a light tea, or in capsules, which can be bought at most health stores, it cures insomnia, migraine headaches, and is a general sedative. Some people are very vulnerable to valerian, and the sedative qualities are stronger than normal. Test your client with a small amount of the tea before permitting a full cup.

Vanilla: peace, calm, beauty, love, and soothing to the spirit. If you want to use it as a massage oil, use the extract sold in your grocery's cooking aisle and dilute it with an unscented lotion. Faeries prize vanilla beans.

Vervain: brings love, contentment, and helps the patient focus mentally while healing. Parts of the plant are poisonous.

Violet: helps in healing open wounds. The scent is romantic, cheering, and helps bring on a light sleep.

White Willow Bark: mild pain killer and fever reducer. The bark contains salicylic acid, or what we normally call aspirin. Do not give white willow bark tea to anyone who is not able to take aspirin.

Wormwood: a cannabis that damages kidneys; possible carcinogenic. Banned from food products in the United States, it may still be purchased as a raw herb.

Yarrow: causes sweating to break a fever, but be cautious of dehydration.

Appendix C: Basic Medical Terminology for the Faery Shaman

As with any specialized area of study, medicine and herbal medicine have vocabularies that novices need to learn as soon as possible. As you move into more sophisticated areas, books, people, and faery will be using some of the following terms to refer to various treatments.

Alterative: A medicine that produces positive change without noticeable side effects.

Anodyne: Pain reliever.

Antacid: Reduces bile in the stomach and esophagus, sometimes stops esophageal contractions.

Anthelmintic: Expels parasites from digestive tract.

Aperiment: Acts as a gentle laxative.

Aromatic: Uses scent to heal, to alter ambient vibrations, or to change mood.

Antigen: Builds antibodies. A vaccine is an antigen.

Antianxiety: Promotes relaxation in situations where anxiety affects the daily life; also used in low dosages over a longer period to treat panic attacks and general anxiety disorders.

Antibilious: Relieves acid reflux, stomach aches, and soothes pancreatic fluids.

Antibiotic: Kills dangerous bacteria inside or outside of the body. Antibiotics do not work on viral ailments unless the virus has left part of the body infected with bacteria. An example is a sinus infection that is a result of viral influenza. Overuse of antibiotics is resulting in antibiotic resistance in some bacteria. Use only when needed and do not stop until the full recommended dosage is complete. This could result in only the least hearty of the bacteria being killed off, paving the way for a new superstrain of bacteria to flourish.

Antidepressant: Attempts to regulate brain chemicals and neurotransmitters that may be causing a variety of symptoms such as profound sadness, insomnia, anxiety, and poor appetite.

Antidote: A remedy for a specific type of poisoning.

Antiemetic: Stops vomiting.

Antihistamine: Blocks the production of histamines triggered by respiratory or contact allergies.

Antileptic: Prevents or stops seizures.

Anti-inflammatory: Ingested to decrease inflammation in various body systems.

Anthilic: Helps prevent the formation of stones or crystals in the urinary tract.

Antirheumatic: Eases the pain of arthritis or other joint pain.

Antiseptic: Prevents or cures bacterial infection.

Antipyretic: A fever reducer.

Antispasmodic: Relieves the pain of spasms or muscle cramps.

Astringent: Causes skin and muscles to contract to stop any discharge.

Cardioactive: Speeds up the heart; can cause arrhythmia or heart failure regardless of what the herb was meant to treat.

Carminative: Relieves gas pressure in the digestive tract.

Cathartic: Cleans out the lower digestive tract by expelling the contents of the large intestines.

Coagulant: Promotes the clotting of blood. Use coagulants externally unless you are a licensed medical professional. A little bleeding is good and can help clean a wound. All wounds should be thoroughly cleaned before being treated by any other method. Improper use of coagulants could result in dangerous blood clots forming inside the venous system of your client.

Demulcent: Reduces visible inflammation. Use externally only.

Diaphoretic: Causing perspiration, can also lead to dehydration.

Discutient: Medicine to stop the growth of tumors, to cure or to prevent tumors.

Diuretic: Increases urine output, but may lead to dehydration.

Emitic: Induces vomiting.

Emmenagogue: Promotes the start of a menstrual period, contains hormones that should be used under supervision.

Emollient: Soothes inflamed skin.

Emulsifier: Promotes digestion and helps regulate bowel movements.

Expectorant: Promotes vomiting or the expulsion of phlegm from the chest.

Febrifugic: Reduces fever.

Hypnotic: Promotes a very deep sleep.

Infectious: An illness likely to produce a bacteria infection; also used interchangeably with the word contagious, which is a commutable disease of bacterial or viral origin.

Laxative: Stimulates the large intestine.

Nauseant: Induces vomiting.

Nervine: A calmative.

Opthalmicum: Medical treatments for the eyes.

Pectoral: Treats chest ailments.

Poultice: A pack of damp and usually warm herbs, carefully wrapped and placed on the skin to draw out illness, break up congestion, or ease pain.

Refrigerant: Cools the body's internal temperature, or one specific part of skin if used externally.

Resolvent: Shrinks boils, tumors, and warts; an archaic term for cancer treatments.

Rebifacient: Speeds circulation and brings blood to the outer layer of the skin. This is what happens during the Pagan ritual of scourging, where one is lightly whipped with leather straps.

Sedative: A calmative that can induce relaxation and sleep.

Stomachic: Word not often used today, but was popular when home remedies were more reliable than medical treatment. Today some people use it to refer to a medicine that relieves symptoms of indigestion.

Styptic: Stops skin surface bleeding.

Sudorific: Induces profuse perspiration. Must be used with the guidance and knowledge of a licensed medical professional; clients may risk severe dehydration, and damage to the liver and kidneys.

Tonic: A general restorative to produce vigor and a brighter mood.

Select Bibliography

A great many books, recorded and printed meditations, and thousands of shared experiences went into the shaping of this book. Not all the works listed here were consulted or cited during the creation of this book, but all contributed in some way to my understanding of faery and its enchantments. I am quite sure that many more books and a multitude of experiences are waiting for me to continue my faery lessons.

The books marked with an asterisk (*) are those I feel are most helpful to the faery shaman seeking a deeper understanding of the world of faery. Many more fine texts and teachers are available to help guide you to be the best faery shaman possible.

Aburrow, Yvonne. *The Enchanted Forest: The Magical Lore of Trees*. Chieveley, UK: Capall Bann Press, 1993.

Andrews, Ted. *Animal Speak: The Spiritual & Magical Powers of Creatures Great & Small*. St. Paul, MN: Llewellyn Publications, 1993.

*_____. *Nature-Speak: Signs, Omens & Messages in Nature*. Jackson, TN: Dragonhawk Publishing, 2004.

Arrowsmith, Nancy and George Moorse. *A Field Guide to the Little People*. New York: Hill and Wang (A Division of Farrar, Straus and Giroux), 1977.

Bartlett, Richard, D.C., Ph.D. *Matrix Energetics: The Art and Science of Transformation*. New York: Atria Books, 2007.

*Blamires, Steve. *Glamoury: Magic of the Celtic Green World*. St. Paul, MN: Llewellyn Publications, 1995.

Bord, Janet. *Fairies: Real Encounters with Little People*. New York: Dell, 1997.

Briggs, Katherine. *The Vanishing People: Fairy Lore and Legends.* New York: Pantheon Books, 1978.

Campbell, Joseph. *The Masks of God: Primitive Mythology.* New York: Viking Press, 1959.

Carmichael, Alexander, ed. *Carmina Gaedelica: Hymns and Incantations from the Gaelic.* Edinburgh, UK: Floris Books, 2004.

Colum, Padriac. *A Treasury of Irish Folklore.* New York: Bonanza Books (A Division of Crown Publishers, Inc.), 1967.

*Conway, D. J. *The Ancient Art of Faery Magick.* Berkeley, CA: Crossing Press, 2005.

_____. *Magickal Mermaids and Water Creatures: Invoke the Magick of the Waters.* Franklin Lakes, NJ: New Page Books, 2005.

Cowan, David and Chris Arnold. *Ley Lines and Earth Energies: A Groundbreaking Exploration of the Earth's Natural Energy and How It Affects Our Health.* Kempton, IL: Adventures Unlimited Press, 2003.

Cowan, Tom. *Shamanism: As a Spiritual Practice for Daily Life.* Berkeley, CA: Crossing Press, 1996.

Cunningham, Scott. *Cunningham's Encyclopedia of Magical Herbs.* St. Paul, MN: Llewellyn Publications, 1986.

_____. *Earth Power: Techniques of Natural Magic.* St. Paul, MN: Llewellyn Publications, 1987.

_____. *Earth, Air, Fire and Water: More Techniques of Natural Magic.* St. Paul, MN: Llewellyn, 1991.

Datlow, Ellen and Terri Windling, eds. *The Fairy Reel: Tales from the Twilight Realm.* New York: Viking, 2004.

Dubois, Pierre. (Claudine and Roland Sabatier, illus.) *The Great Encyclopedia of Faeries.* New York: Simon & Schuster, 1999.

Duffy, Maureen. The *Erotic World of Faery.* London: Sphere Books, Ltd., 1989.

Dumars, Denise and Lori Nyx. *The Dark Archetype: Exploring the Shadow Side of the Divine.* Franklin Lakes, NJ: New Page Books, 2003.

Eliade, Mircea. *Shamanism: Archaic Techniques of Ecstasy.* Princeton, NJ: The Princeton University Press, 1964.

*Evans-Wentz, W. Y. *The Fairy Faith in Celtic Countries.* New York: University Books, 1966 (Containing oral histories and personal experiences collected by the author in the late ninteenth century, first published in 1911 as *The Fairy Mythology*).

Farrar, Janet and Stewart, and Gavin Bone. *The Healing Craft: Healing Practices for Witches and Pagans*. Blaine, WA: Phoenix Publishing, Inc., 1999.

*Foxwood, Orion. *The Faery Teachings*. Coral Springs, FL: Muse Press, 2003.

Franklin, Anna. *Working with Faeries*. Franklin Lakes, NJ: New Page Books, 2006.

Franklin, Anna and Paul Mason. *Guide to the Fairy Ring*. St. Paul, MN: Llewellyn Publications, 2002.

Froud, Brain and Alan Lee. (Edited and Illustrated by David Larkin.) *Faeries*. New York: Harry N. Abrams, 1978.

*Froud, Brian and Jessica MacBeth. *The Faeries Oracle: Working with the Faeries to Find Insight, Wisdom, and Joy*. New York: Simon & Schuster, 2000.

Froud, Brian. (Terri Windling, ed.) *Good Faeries, Bad Faeries*. New York: Simon & Schuster, 1998.

Geddes-Ward, Alicen and Neil. *FaerieCraft: Treading the Path of Faerie Magic*. Carlsbad, CA: Hay House, 2005.

Guiley, Rosemary Ellen. *Fairy Magic*. London: Element Books, 2004.

*Harner, Michael. *The Way of the Shaman*. San Francisco: Harper-San Francisco (tenth anniversary edition), 1990.

Hazlitt, W. Carew. *Faiths and Folklore of the British Isles (Volumes I and II)*. New York: Benjamin Blom, 1965.

*Heaven, Ross and Howard G. Charing. *Plant Spirit Shamanism*. Rochester, VT: Destiny Books, 2006.

Hodson, Geoffrey. *Fairies at Work and at Play*. London: The Theosophical Publishing House, 1982.

Hoffman, David. *The Complete Illustrated Holistic Herbal: A Safe and Practical Guide to Making and Using Herbal Remedies*. Shaftesbury, Dorset, UK: Element Books, 1996.

Huygen, Wil. *Gnomes* (Translated from the Dutch). New York: Peacock Press (A Division of Bantam Books), 1977.

Keightley, Thomas. *The World Guide to Gnomes, Fairies, Elves and Other Little People*. New York: Avenel Books, 1978 (Originally published in 1880 as *The Fairy Mythology*).

Knight, Sirona. *Faery Magick: Spells, Potions, and Lore from the Earth Spirits*. Franklin Lakes, NJ: New Page Books, 2002.

Lawless, Julia. *The Illustrated Encyclopedia of Essential Oils*. Shaftesbury, Dorset, UK: Element Books, 1995.

Lenihan, Edmund. *In Search of Biddy Early*. Dublin: Mercier Press, 1987.

Matthews, Caitín and John. *The Encyclopedia of Celtic Wisdom*. Shaftesbury, Dorset, UK: Element Books, 1994.

*_____. *Walkers Between the Worlds: The Western Mysteries from Shaman to Magus*. Rochester, VT: Inner Traditions, 2004.

Matthews, John. *The Celtic Shaman*. Shaftesbury, Dorset, UK: Earth Quest, 1991.

_____. *The Sidhe: Wisdom from the Celtic Otherworld*. Issaquah, WA: The Lorian Association, 2004.

*McArthur, Margie. *Faery Healing: The Lore and the Legacy*. Aptos, CA: New Brighton Books, 2003.

McCoy, Edain. *A Witch's Guide to Faery Folk*. St. Paul, MN: Llewellyn Publications, 1994.

Macowen, Frank Henderson. *The Spiral of Memory and Belonging: A Celtic Path of Soul and Kinship*. New York: New American Library, 2004.

Miller, Richard Alan and Iona Miller. *The Magical and Ritual Use of Perfumes*. Rochester, VT: Destiny Books, 1990.

Mynne, Hugh. *The Faerie Way*. St. Paul, MN: Llewellyn Publications, 1996.

Penczak, Christopher. *Ascension Magick*. Woodbury, MN: Llewellyn Publications, 2007.

_____. *The Temple of Shamanic Witchcraft: Shadows, Spirits and the Healing Journey*. St. Paul, MN: Llewellyn Publications, 2005.

*Pennick, Nigel. *Celtic Sacred Landscapes*. London: Thames and Hudson, 2000.

Robertson, R. MacDonald. *Selected Highland Folktales*. London: David and Charles (Second Edition), 1977.

Rose, Carol. *Spirits, Fairies, Leprechauns, and Goblins: An Encyclopedia.* New York: W.W. Norton & Co., 1996.

Scott, Allan and Michael Scott Rohan. *Fantastic People: Magical Races of Myth and Legend.* New York: Galahad Books, 1980.

*Stewart, R. J. *Earth Light: The Ancient Path to Transformation Rediscovering the Wisdom of Celtic & Faery Lore.* North Carolina: Mercury Publishing, 1998.

*_____. *The Spirit Cord.* United Kingdom: R.J. Stewart Books, 2006.

*_____, (Sarah Lever, illustrator). *The Living World of Faery.* North Carolina: Mercury Publishing, 1999.

*_____. *The Underworld Initiation: A Journey Towards Psychic Transformation (Celtic Myth & Legend, Vol. 3).* North Carolina: Mercury Publishing, 1998.

*_____. *The Well of Light: From Faery Healing to Earth Healing.* Scotland: R. J. Stewart Books, 2007.

Tiller, William A., Ph.D.; Dibble, Walter E., Jr., Ph.D.; and Micheal J. Kohane, Ph.D. *Conscious Acts of Creation: The Emergence of a New Physics.* Walnut Creek, CA: Pavior Publishing, 1997.

Whitmont, Edward, M.D. *The Alchemy of Healing: Psyche and Soma.* Berkeley, CA: North Atlantic Books, 1993.

Index

About the Author

Edain McCoy became a self-initiated Witch in 1981 and underwent a formal initiation in 1983 with a large San Antonio coven. She began researching alternative spiritualities in her teens and has worked with teachings of Kabbalah, the Celts, Appalachia, Curanderismo, Eclectic Wicca, Jewitchery, and Faery Shamanism. In Irish Witta she is a Priestess of Brighid and an Elder. She loves the North American Pagan Festivals, equating them to a great summer camp she hates to leave. Much of her research focus has shifted toward the syncretic spiritual traditions of the Americas, which she believes have moved away from their roots in Western European practice to become unique expressions of American Paganism. She hopes her annual sojourns to Argentina will result in getting her feet in the door of the secretive sect of Candomblé with the help of Wiccan friends in Buenos Aires, and to unravel other paranormal mysteries and offer tours to ghostly sites with her South American partners at TangoWithJudy.com. In 2006 Edain founded Pisces Moon Paranormal, a small group of multiskilled investigators seeking the secrets behind ghosts, apparitions, and other anomalous occurrences. Contact her through *www.EdainMcCoy.com*.